THE AUTHOR Christopher
Traveller's History of England, which has a strong international leader......,
twenty-five years he lived and worked in York and was for many years the
editor of the journal of the York Archaeological Trust. He was a committee
member of the Yorkshire Architectural and York Archaeological Society, The
Rowntree Society and is currently an Honorary Visiting Fellow in the Centre
for Medieval Studies, a department of the University of York. He is now a
Historic Building Advisor for Defence Estates.

SERIES EDITOR Professor Denis Judd is a graduate of Oxford, a Fellow of
the Royal Historical Society and Professor of History at the London Metropolitan University. He has published over 20 books including the biographies
of Joseph Chamberlain, Prince Philip, George VI and Alison Uttley, historical
and military subjects, stories for children and two novels. His most recent books
are the highly praised *Empire: The British Imperial Experience from 1765 to the
Present* and (with Keith Surridge) *The Boer War*. He has reviewed and written
extensively in the national press and in journals and is an advisor to the BBC
History Magazine.

Other Titles in the Series

A Traveller's History of Athens
A Traveller's History of Australia
A Traveller's History of Canada
A Traveller's History of China
A Traveller's History of the
  Caribbean
A Traveller's History of Cyprus
A Traveller's History of England
A Traveller's History of France
A Traveller's History of Germany
A Traveller's History of Greece
A Traveller's History of the Hundred
  Years War
A Traveller's History of India
A Traveller's History of Ireland
A Traveller's History of Italy
A Traveller's History of Japan

A Traveller's History of London
A Traveller's History of Mexico
A Traveller's History of New Zealand
  and the South Pacific Islands
A Traveller's History of North Africa
A Traveller's History of Oxford
A Traveller's History of Paris
A Traveller's History of Portugal
A Traveller's History of Scotland
A Traveller's History of South Africa
A Traveller's History of South East
  Asia
A Traveller's History of Spain
A Traveller's History of Turkey
A Traveller's History of the USA
A Traveller's History of Venice

THE TRAVELLER'S HISTORY SERIES

A Traveller's History of York

To my wife
Alison

A Traveller's History of York

CHRISTOPHER DANIELL

Series Editor DENIS JUDD
Line drawings PETER GEISSLER
Maps JOHN TAYLOR

CHASTLETON TRAVEL
An imprint of Arris Publishing Ltd
Gloucestershire

First published in Great Britain in 2006
by Chastleton Travel
An imprint of Arris Publishing Ltd
12 Adlestrop, Moreton in Marsh
Gloucestershire GL56 0YN
www.arrisbooks.com

Text copyright © Christopher Daniell 2006
Preface copyright © Denis Judd 2006
Line drawings by Peter Geissler
Maps by John Taylor

The front cover shows a north-west view of York Minster by Frederic Mackenzie, York Museums Trust (York Art Gallery) The Bridgeman Art Library

ISBN 1-905214-03-0
ISBN 13 978-1-905214-03-7

Typeset by DP Photosetting, Aylesbury, Bucks
Printed and bound in Great Britain by William Clowes Ltd, Beccles, Suffolk

Telephone: 01608 659328
Visit our website at www.arrisbooks.com or email us at info@arrisbooks.com

Contents

Preface

Very few British cities can rival York for the richness and length of its history. Very many significant episodes in Britain during the past two thousand years have had their 'York dimension'. Not merely that, but the name has been exported throughout the English-speaking world by settlers and migrants, and by one Duke of York in particular; in the United States, there is not merely New York, but also over twenty 'other' Yorks; Canada has Yorkton and York Factory; and Australia has one York, a Cape York and Yorketown, there are three in the former British West Indies, two in South Africa and, significantly, two in the formerly freed slave colony of Sierra Leone.

Where did it all begin? For the answer to this, and to many other questions, the curious can now pick up Christopher Daniell's concise, learned, very readable and comprehensive history. Nobody is better placed to write this book than Christopher Daniell, who lived for twenty-five years in the city, serving on various local archaeological committees, and who is currently an Honorary Visiting Fellow in the Centre for Medieval Studies at the University of York.

York's geographical position was the making of the city. Situated at the conjunction of two rivers, the Ouse that flows towards the Humber and the North Sea and the smaller Foss, which allowed travel north, and then eastwards, the site could also be easily defended. Not surprisingly, the Romans saw its advantages as a military strong point and in 71 AD established the fortified settlement of Eboracum – a name that probably means 'the place of the yew trees'. From 211 AD York became the provincial capital of the Roman province of Lower Britain. Eboracum also saw several dramatic passages of imperial Roman history, for not only did two Emperors (Septimus Severus and Constantine Chlorus) die there, but the later Constantine was proclaimed at York.

In a way, therefore, even before the coming of the Anglo-Saxons, Christianity, or the Vikings, York's position as a northern capital was settled. Its relative proximity to the independent and often troublesome region of Scotland also helped to confirm its value as a major northern bastion of English power. In due course it was to become the seat of the second archbishopric after Canterbury, a centre of revolt against William the Conqueror, the place of the infamous 1190 massacre of almost the entire Jewish community, the site of Edward I's exchequer and chancery, the venue for the marriage of King Edward III and Philippa of Hainault, the city where Dick Turpin was hanged, the target of three German Zeppelin raids in 1916 and heavy Luftwaffe bombing in 1942, and much else besides.

The name can be found in many other situations. There is 'the grand old Duke of York', the York Mystery Plays, the Yorkist faction in the Wars of the Roses – which produced the two Yorkist Kings Edward IV and Richard III – the 'yorker' ball in cricket, the National Railway Museum at York, and of course the sublime York Minster.

Today York is a greater magnet for visitors than ever before, and it clearly thrives on it. In the centre, its streets, many as picturesque and ancient as the Shambles, boast not merely fine shops but an increasingly sophisticated range of restaurants and eating-places. Whether the visitor has arrived in York for a day trip or for a lengthier stay, the city will beguile, inspire and please in equal measure. A reading of Christopher Daniell's excellent new book will certainly enhance this delightful experience.

Denis Judd
London, 2005

CHAPTER ONE

Origins – Prehistoric and Roman York

For thousands of years York has been a focus for human activity. The importance of the location has been created as a result of the underlying geology of the region. The geology of Yorkshire can be broadly understood as a progression from older rocks of the central Pennines and then progressively newer rocks towards the coast.

The oldest Pennine rocks were laid down during the Carboniferous period (between 280–345 million years ago) which include sandstone and coal, the coal being the fossilised trees from the swamps which covered the region. The youngest deposits are those of the Cretaceous period (144 – 65 million years ago), during which time a warm shallow sea covered East Yorkshire. The animals in the sea died and fell to the bottom, and over time thick chalk deposits were laid down which today form the undulating Wolds. The range of the different under-lying rocks of the region has resulted in a wide variation of landscapes within Yorkshire, from the high bleak Pennines, to the flat alluvial Vale of York, to the rolling chalk wolds of east Yorkshire.

More recently the underlying geology has been moulded and altered over the last 435,000 years by the successive advances and retreats of ice during the Ice Ages. The glaciers and ice sheets scoured the upland landscape and deposited material during its retreat.

The last glaciation, which occurred about 18,000 years ago, had a profound effect upon York's landscape. At its furthest point south the ice sheet reached the Doncaster area (about forty miles from York) but when it was melting the ice sheet stopped for a while just south of the

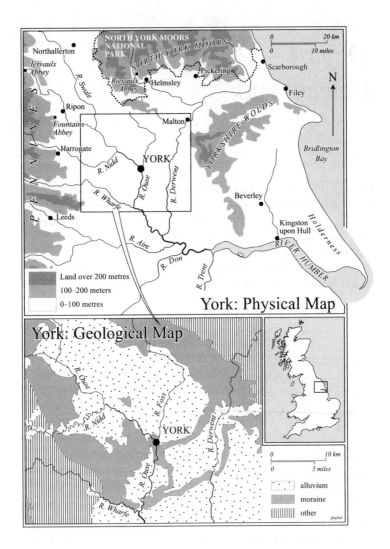

York: Physical Map

York: Geological Map

city. The glaciers and ice sheets have the effect of a conveyer belt, grinding up the underlying rocks and carrying the resultant boulders, stones and clay to the edge, where they are deposited. If the glacier does not retreat or advance the accumulating debris forms into long ridges at the glacier's edge, which are known as terminal moraines. It is the York moraine which forms the high point of the landscape around York, forming a ridge to the south-east of the city near the present day university. Another result of the moraines was that they trapped the water from the melting glaciers. The resultant lake, Lake Pickering, was almost thirty miles long and up to ten miles wide.

The second effect of the last glaciation was that as the ice sheets melted the present day river systems began to form. The glaciation was responsible for one of the most remarkable river courses in England. The River Derwent passes just five miles from the North Sea coast. Before the last ice age it flowed directly into the North Sea but the glaciers blocked its former route and so the river turned inland and now travels nearly a hundred miles southwards, past York and into the Humber estuary.

Evidence of animals living during the ice age and prehistoric times have been found in caves at Kirkdale in North Yorkshire. There are two theories as to how the animal bones came to be in the caves. The first is that hyenas dragged dead animals into their den during the warmer periods of the ice age. The finds include the bones of straight-tusked elephant, rhinoceros, hippopotamus, bison and giant deer. Other bones, indicative of a colder climate, were found, such as those of reindeer, and horse, but they were found in a layer of silt. This has resulted in the second theory that dead animals may have been washed into the cave when the area was flooded by the enormous Lake Pickering.

The last ice age therefore created the present day topography around York. The combination of the moraines and river courses meant that York's location became a nodal point of communication throughout history. The River Ouse created the largest river valley in the north of England, some twenty-five miles wide, between the Pennines and the Wolds, and the higher terminal moraines meant easy routeways across areas of wetlands.

The Stone Age

The Stone Age is traditionally split into three periods of time: paleolithic (the Old Stone Age, 'paleo' meaning 'old', 'lithic' meaning 'stone'), mesolithic (Middle Stone Age) and neolithic (New Stone Age).

As the ice retreated and the conditions became more habitable people began to move northwards and settle in the region. Initially Yorkshire seems to have been the furthest north that paleolithic peoples travelled. Isolated finds, such as a group of flints or an antler harpoon, indicate small groups of people travelling to the region on hunting trips, and then returning to the warmer southern areas.

During the mesolithic era the ice sheets retreated further north and there is increasing evidence of people, especially in the uplands of the North York Moors area. However, it is around the low lying shores of Lake Pickering that one of the most famous mesolithic sites in England has been discovered, at Starr Carr. There is bone evidence at the site of domesticated dogs, as well as animals which were eaten such as red deer, elk, ox and pigs. The site was probably a seasonal hunting camp which was occupied in the late spring and summer.

The neolithic people living in Yorkshire are difficult to trace because there is little evidence for their settlements, despite the fact that it is in the neolithic period that people changed from being nomadic hunter-gatherers to farmers of the land. Whilst their settlements are scarce, there is much more evidence for the burial and ritual sites. There are two main types of burial sites: long barrows (which have long elongated rectangular shapes) and round barrows, either of which forms could be several metres in height. The long barrows are spread across the North York Moors and the Wolds whilst the round barrows are concentrated in the Wolds area to the north-east of York. Often the barrows had many phases of use and a common pattern was that a few bodies were buried in them at first, and then later the original bodies were moved or additional artefacts were put into the barrow. One of the largest round barrows is at Duggelby Howe and grave goods included boars' tusks, a flint knife, arrowheads and bone pins.

Whilst the long and round barrows lie to the north and east of York, to the north-west and west lie a remarkable series of ritual henges, which are circular enclosures with an internal ditch and external bank. The largest is the Thornborough Circles which are three massive henges situated north of Ripon. Like many neolithic monuments their use and meaning is unclear, but it has recently been suggested that the three circles have the same formation as the belt of Orion, one of the major constellations visible in the winter night sky.

Neolithic evidence has been discovered in York in the form of twenty-three polished axes – the largest number found anywhere in the Vale of York. Also in York a unique hoard of flint implements was discovered in 1868 during building works. The flints were in a pit 'that could be covered by a man's hat' and consisted of seven axes, two arrowheads, three scrapers, nine knives or spearheads, blades and an arrowhead. These are unlikely to be from a settlement site, but rather an individual probably buried them for safe keeping. Indeed, none of the neolithic finds from York indicate a permanent settlement, but the sheer number indicate that York was a key site for neolithic people travelling to other areas.

Bronze Age

Around 2,000 BC a technological revolution occurred: for the first time in England objects began to be made of metal – gold, silver and bronze – rather than just stone or wood. The wide spread use of bronze to make axes, knives and ornaments has resulted in the era becoming known as the Bronze Age. The evidence for Bronze Age people in Yorkshire is predominantly their burials. Whereas neolithic people tended to have several people in a single grave, during the Bronze Age the burial of individuals in round barrows became more common. In the Yorkhire Wolds there are over 1,400 Bronze Age round barrows and many are grouped together in cemeteries. Even thousands of years later some are still clearly visible in the landscape.

As well as the technological changes during the Bronze Age there were also climatic changes with more rainfall and a cooler climate. There was also a rise in sea level making it possible to navigate far upstream along the Yorkshire rivers from the Humber estuary and the

North Sea. The bronze coming into the region shows that trade was taking place and remarkably three Bronze Age boats have been discovered at North Ferriby which lies on the shores of the Humber estuary. The boats were able to cross the North Sea or English Channel, and could also journey up the Humber and the other rivers. The boats were rowed and were large enough to carry animals as well as people. Further fragments have been found on the estuary and so more boats may wait to be discovered.

In York there are tantalising clues to significant Bronze Age activity, though unfortunately much of the evidence was found in previous centuries and was either not recorded or is now lost. As well as three burials discovered in York, there are also many items, such as axes and a spearhead, though in comparison with other areas of the country there is a noticeable lack of swords.

The Iron Age

Like the Bronze Age, the Iron Age is marked by the introduction of new technology which meant that iron, a harder and more practically useful metal than the softer bronze, began to be produced in quantity. Iron Age sites are scattered widely across Yorkshire, both in the upland areas and also in the lower, more fertile, Vale of York. From a combination of archaeological and historical records it is known that there were two main tribes in Iron Age Yorkshire, the Brigantes in West Yorkshire and the Pennines, and the Parisi in East Yorkshire.

THE PARISI

Towards the Yorkshire coast, in the area now approximating to the East Riding of Yorkshire, was a relatively small Iron Age tribe called the Parisi. The tribal name is from the same derivation as that of 'Paris', the capital of France, and so it is possible that the Parisi of East Yorkshire migrated to the region from the Champagne region of France. However, East Yorkshire is not an obvious location for people from France, and it may be that there were marriages or dynastic links between the regions. It is suspected that the capital of the Parisi, which the Romans called 'Petvaria' was at the present day Brough on

Humber. The name Petvaria is derived from the Celtic 'petuario' meaning 'fourth', suggesting that the tribe had four divisions within their territory.

The Parisi have left spectacular objects as part of their burial rituals. The most extraordinary of these is where an individual is buried with an entire chariot. Many are known from the wolds, and a recent example has been excavated at Wetwang. The burial was of a woman in her thirties, and the presence of the chariot shows that women were capable of being powerful in Iron Age societies. Also buried with her was an iron mirror. The mirror was decorated with coral which could only have come from the Mediterranean or beyond. The burial was dated to 2300 years old (700 BC). These chariot burials are largely confined to East Yorkshire (though one has been found near Edinburgh) but chariot burials are also found in the Arras region (Belgium and northern France) which also shows a link between the regions.

THE BRIGANTES

The single largest Iron Age tribal group in the north was the Brigantes, a loose federation of tribes covering the north of England. The name of the Brigantes has several possible derivations: the word 'briga' or 'brica' was sometimes used to signify a town or settlement; it may mean 'the high one' (possibly because of the mountainous area they lived in) but more likely the 'Briga-' prefix refers to the Celtic goddess Brigit. Therefore the name probably means 'the people of Brigit'.

Nothing is known about the personalities or rulers of the Brigantes before the Romans arrived but enough remains physically for archaeologists to be able to piece together how the Brigantes lived. Settlements of the Brigantes and other Iron Age tribes have been found scattered across the countryside. The Iron Age families or communities lived in circular wooden huts often within a ditched enclosure. Today the outlines of these huts can sometimes be seen from the air, or alternatively some have remained prominent enough for unwary walkers to trip over them. The stone outlines of such huts can clearly be seen either on Ilkley Moor or on the top of Ingleborough, one of the high peaks in the Yorkshire Dales.

As well as the houses, archaeologists have discovered other structures, such as pits which were lined and sealed to preserve food,
buildings which may have been for corn storage, small ovens for baking
bread and enclosures for keeping cattle. Before the Romans the concept and use of money was unknown to the Brigantes and they
probably measured their wealth in terms of precious metals or cattle.

The Romans Arrive

The Romans invaded England three times, the first two times were by
Julius Caesar in consecutive years in 55 and 54 BC. The first invasion
was brief and only affected the southern part of the country. Caesar left
and returned better prepared the following summer. This time the
Romans marched further inland and defeated one of the most
important of the native kings, Cassivellaunus, who thus becomes the
first named native British historical figure. Following this victory Caesar
once again left and Britain was free from Roman rule for another
hundred years.

In AD 43 the Romans once again attacked, but this time they had
more permanent intentions. From their landing place in Kent the
Romans fanned out northwards and southwards and soon gained
control of most of southern England. In AD 43 there was a great
ceremony of surrender by the native chiefs to the Emperor Claudius at
Colchester. Although the names of those who surrendered are not
known, it is quite possible that it included the chiefs of the Brigantes
and Parisi tribes.

In the early fifties the leader of the Brigantes tribe was a queen called
Cartimandua. Cartimandua is one of only two Celtic women to be
mentioned in contemporary Roman sources – the other was her more
famous contemporary Boudicca who rose up in revolt and devastated
several major towns, such as Verulamium (present day St Albans) and
London itself. It is known that Cartimandua took as her consort
Venutius, the chief of the Carvetii tribe which was one of the stronger
tribes in the Brigantes federation. The couple made a powerful pair as
Cartimandua's powerbase was probably at Barwick in Elmet in West
Yorkshire, whilst Venutius' powerbase was in the north and he con-

trolled one of the most important strongholds of the Brigantes at Stanwick in North Yorkshire.

At first the tribes which made up the Brigantes tribal group were of little military concern to the Romans as the invaders concentrated on conquering the south and Midland areas of England. However, following common practice, the Romans made tribes on the borders of their conquered territory 'client states', with the result that the Romans effectively ruled tribes whilst leaving local rulers in place.

Even though there were minor revolts against Roman control by rebellious groups within the Brigantes federation, they were not particularly serious. However, as a result of the Welsh campaigns by the Romans the chief of the Catuvellaunian tribe, Caratacus, fled to Cartimandua's court in AD 51. At this point Cartimandua's loyalties became seriously divided between Rome and Rome's enemy Caratacus.

Caught between intense Roman pressure and tribal loyalties, Cartimandua handed Caratacus over to the Roman governor of Britannia – a rich political prize for the Romans. Caratacus and his family were taken in chains to Rome, but there his proud bearing and refusal to be cowed impressed even the Emperor Claudius and Caratacus was allowed to live in honourable captivity for the rest of his life.

For her part in his capture, Cartimandua received wealth and rewards from the Romans, but other chiefs of the tribe were resentful. To make matters worse Cartimandua and Venutius became enemies, as a consequence of her taking her own armour-bearer, Vellocatus, as her new consort.

Venutius and his Brigantes followers attacked Cartimandua in AD 53, but with Roman support Cartimandua defeated him. An uneasy stalemate lasted until AD 70 when once again Venutius rose in revolt. The Romans at the time were fighting the Silures tribe of South Wales, but a force was sent to rescue Cartimandua, and the Roman commander annulled the client status of the tribe. Even though technically the Brigantes had lost their client status and were now under direct Roman rule, in practice Venutius was still at large and waging war against Rome. For the time being Romans had lost control in the north.

In the Parisi lands, there is little evidence of revolt, but the Parisi were sandwiched between the Roman presence in the south at Lincoln and the much bigger tribe of the Brigantes to the north and west. However, the Parisi were to prove pivotal to the Roman conquest of the Brigantes.

THE FOUNDING OF EBORACUM: ROMAN YORK IN AD 71

The revolt of the Brigantes and the potential loss of influence in the whole of the north of England was a situation the Romans could not allow to remain unchallenged. In AD 71, the Roman governor of Britain, Quintus Petilius Cerealis, led the Ninth Legion northwards from Lincoln to invade 'Brigantia'.

The Ninth Legion had been one of the original legions to cross to Britain in AD 43 and so were a battle-hardened unit. The Romans bypassed the dangerous heartlands of the Brigantes by crossing the River Humber at Brough and marching through the lands of the Parisi tribe. As the Romans marched and conquered the territory they built a series of forts to protect the soldiers and their supply lines. The forts probably included Brough (to protect the crossing across the River Humber) and Malton, the largest fort on the Yorkshire Wolds. The large fort at Malton was also probably built to control the Parisi tribe.

During the campaign the Roman commander Cerealis recognised that there was a good military strongpoint at the juncture of two rivers, the Ouse and the Foss, and based an army camp there. The site had many advantages. As well as the rivers on two sides, the banks of the River Ouse formed steep cliffs which added to the defensive nature of the site. Communications were also good, because the River Ouse allowed for supplies to be brought or sent from the Humber and out into the North Sea, and the Foss allowed communications towards the east.

The name given to the site was 'Eboracum' which through many changes of spelling and pronunciation has led to the present day name of York. The Roman meaning of Eboracum is unclear, but probably means 'the place of the yew trees'. One of the oddities about the placing of the fort was that there does not seem to have been any pre-existing settlement on the site. It was a common Roman tactic to place forts or settlements alongside or near the principal tribal centres in order to control them. There is no evidence – either written or archaeo-logical – that there was any existing Iron Age tribal settlement. However the choice of the location is interesting because it was on the borders of both the Parisi tribe to the east, and the Brigantes to the west. The site was therefore a relatively neutral area from which to build a centre of Roman rule, though if both tribes had risen in unison then the Roman fort would have been sandwiched between the two attacking forces. In this case the River Ouse would either have formed a vital supply route for extra troops and supplies, or escape.

With access to the heartlands of the Brigantes' lands and a large, battle-hardened legion, the Romans crushed the rebellion of the Brigantes and thereafter marched north to conquer the rest of the north with comparative ease.

THE LEGIONARY FORTRESS

With a more settled hinterland the initial camp at Eboracum was transformed into a major fortress by the Ninth Legion. The original construction of the first fortress was made of wood and then later from stone. The last record of the legion at York is in AD 107. It is the Ninth Legion that has many myths and stories associated with it. Legend relates that the legion marched north and 'disappeared' as a result of being slaughtered by the native tribes. The truth is more mundane. The Ninth Legion was sent overseas to what is now the Netherlands. One of the last records of the legion is in AD 161 where it may have been wiped out in the wars against the Parthians in the east.

However, unexpectedly, the Ninth Legion reappeared – almost 2000 years later. In 1953 a group of men were working in the cellar of the Treasurer's House in Minster Yard and one, Harry Martindale, was up a ladder fixing a pipe. He heard a trumpet blast and then a horse and rider, and group of soldiers marched through one wall, across the room and through the other wall. Not surprisingly he was so amazed that he fell off his ladder. This is possibly the most famous ghost story in York, and despite the dubiousness of many such stories this one is treated with more credibility than most. Harry and the other men were able to give unusual details of the uniforms which have since turned out to be correct.

After the Ninth Legion left, the Sixth Legion garrisoned the city. Under the Sixth Legion the fortress at York enclosed fifty acres and housed a garrison of several thousand soldiers. Remarkably two references have been found to a single man serving in the Sixth Legion in the north of England. Sollius Julianus commanded a small unit of one hundred men within the Sixth Legion. The first time his name was discovered was on an inscription stating that Marcus Sollius Julianus' men had built a section of Hadrian's Wall. Then, during archaeological excavations in York in the 1980s, a second reference to him and his men was found. A large leather panel was discovered which had originally been a side of a Roman military tent. When cleaned the scratches on the leather revealed that the tent had belonged to the men of Sollius Julianus.

The outline of the Legionary fortress was a playing card shape and in the first century the internal structures of forts across the Roman Empire were standardised to such an extent that the layout of the fort at York can be determined. The single most important building was the *principia* – this was the home of the governor and the administrative heart of the fort, which today lies under York Minster. Around the *principia* were a grid of streets with a main axis of streets running across the front of the *principia* to the two main gateways, imaginatively called in Latin the Principal Gateway Left and the Principal Gateway Right. A street ran from the entrance of the *principia* to the gate facing the river, roughly equating with Stonegate today. Through the gate there was a large bridge crossing the Ouse, and the street then ran in a straight line and exited the city at Micklegate Bar.

Through the centuries the fortress went through many changes in appearance with new buildings and roads being built, though the basic playing card layout of the outer defences was retained. The lack of precise dating evidence for many of these features means that the exact dates of buildings have yet to be determined.

As well as the purely military buildings, there were a wide range of other buildings in which a variety of entertainments took place. There was a large bath house for troops and civilians alike with hot and cold baths. The source of the water has yet to be discovered but it may have been piped in from over twenty miles away. There was also the grand

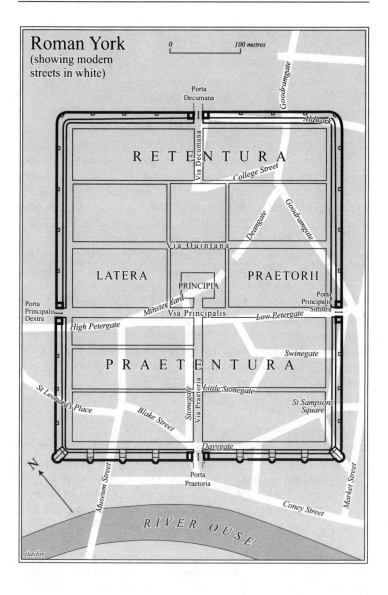

Roman York
(showing modern streets in white)

0   100 metres

spectacle of the games and battles within the amphitheatre. The site of the amphitheatre remains a mystery though a good guess is that it is just outside the legionary fort between the walls and the River Foss. Within the amphitheatre the spectators watched gladiators fight between themselves, or with ferocious wild animals. As well as the grand entertainments, evidence of more modest amusements such as dice and counters, are commonly discovered from Roman York which show that the Romans loved gambling and skilful board games.

Part of Eboracum's importance was that it was large enough not only to have a legionary fortress, but also a large associated civilian settlement called a *colonia*. The *colonia* was across the River Ouse from the fortress and had spread out like the shape of an open fan, inside of which were streets laid out in grids. The limits of the *colonia* can be broadly defined by two factors. The first is that of the presence of cemeteries which had to be away from urban areas, therefore a lack of cemeteries close to the outskirts of urban areas probably indicates buildings. The second factor is that it is assumed that there was an encircling wall around the *colonia*. This wall is one of the great puzzles of Roman Eboracum, for although three sections have been found, they are all in the same short stretch of wall. It is generally assumed, though maybe wrongly, that the later medieval walls follow the line of the Roman walls. Through this supposed wall were a series of known gates, the most important one being on the site of the present day Micklegate Bar.

RELIGION IN YORK

Religion was a powerful force in the Roman Empire and the Romans believed in many gods. Emperors too became gods after their deaths (and were holy whilst living) and so were worshipped widely. The *principia* was the administrative heart of the city, and it was also the location of the legionary shrine which probably contained an image or statue of the current emperor of the time. As well as the emperors, the most important gods were worshipped across the Empire, such as Minerva, goddess of Wisdom and Jupiter and Juno as well as more minor gods including Victory, Fortune and Hercules. Gods could also be worshipped locally. In south-west England at Bath there is a classic example of a common Roman practice of conflating a local god or goddess with a Roman deity. At Bath the Celtic god Sul was joined with the Roman goddess Minerva to create Sulis Minerva who guarded the hot springs at Bath. As the site was a new one at York, with no previous Celtic settlement nor gods, the gods worshipped in York were mostly of purely Roman origin.

INDIVIDUALS

Evidence for individuals connected with York have survived in the form of inscriptions and artefacts, and in some cases the people themselves. The Romans were keen to commemorate themselves and their relatives. The richer members of society built elaborate tombs or erected beautiful gravestones. Until the end of the Roman Empire cemeteries were forbidden within the city walls or in urban areas. Therefore cemeteries were located either along the road sides or in defined spaces away from habitation.

Tombstones often recorded the person's name, rank or occupation and a pious inscription such as that of Julia Brice. Sometimes more than one member of the family was commemorated with a carved and painted picture catching the eye. During the Victorian period many such tombstones were found whilst digging the foundations for the railway station and the best examples are now in the Yorkshire Museum.

One of the finest tombstones commemorates Julia Velva, which was found on The Mount in 1922. The image on the gravestone shows Julia as the centre of attention and she is reclining whilst eating a meal. To recline whilst eating was a mark of both wealth and age, for only those adults rich enough reclined: children and servants ate at table. Also in the scene are two children standing by a table whilst to the right is a man, presumably her husband, who is named on the tombstone as Aurelius Merculialis. This is a charming picture of a family, and one of the children even holds a pet bird.

In the Roman cemeteries the people themselves still sometime survive. It is unfortunate that centuries later the building campaigns of the Victorians decimated many of the Roman cemeteries. Only fragments of the numerous Roman cemeteries now survive, but even so the skeletal evidence discovered allows an appreciation of the people

D.   M.
IVLIE BRICE AN XXXI
SEPRONIE MARTINE AN VI
SEPRONVS MRINVS F.C.

The Roman tombstone of Julia Brice, aged 31, and her daughter Sempronia
Martina, aged 6. The mother holds an urn and her child a pet bird

themselves. One cemetery was excavated at Trentholme Drive, which
contained 342 burials and 53 cremations. (Cremation was commonly
used at the beginning of the Roman period and then burial became
more popular.) The people buried were not much shorter than today's
average, with the men averaging 1.70 m (5ft 7in) and the women
1.55m (5ft 1in). Arthritis was a common ailment and life expectancy
was short, with 75 per cent of people dying before they were forty years
old. Usually there is a normal ratio of men and women in cemeteries,
but at Trentholme Drive there are, puzzlingly, four times as many men
as women.

There is one extraordinary piece of evidence from the early years of
Eboracum's existence of a Greek visitor. During the creation of the

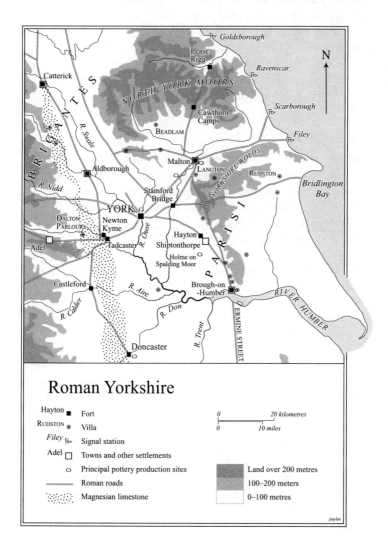

Roman Yorkshire

Hayton ■	Fort		
RUDSTON ⊙	Villa		
Filey ⌐	Signal station		
Adel □	Towns and other settlements		
○	Principal pottery production sites		
——	Roman roads		
⋰⋰⋰	Magnesian limestone		

0 ———— 20 kilometres
0 ———— 10 miles

Land over 200 metres
100–200 meters
0–100 metres

railway station two bronze plaques were discovered dedicated in Greek by Scribonius Demetrius. One plaque was to 'the gods of the military commander's residence' and the other to 'Ocean and Tethys' who were gods of the Greek creation myth. This is extraordinary in itself, but the story takes a new twist as Scribonius seems to have been a traveller and returned to his native Greece where, at Delphi, he met the writer Plutarch, who mentions Scribonius's journey to the 'western isles'.

THE COUNTRYSIDE

York was the hub of Roman life in the north. However Roman presence and culture was also dominant in the more fertile countryside and other towns in the region. The initial Roman need to conquer the region had resulted in a large number of forts, which in turn stimulated the growth of civilian settlements to supply goods for the soldiers. Another important Roman settlement in Yorkshire was Aldborough, which was the civilian administrative centre for the Brigantes tribe. There was also a widespread distribution of forts and their associated settlements. The forts and towns were supplied by a network of villas producing meat and grain. Some villas were wealthy enough to have high class mosaics such as Rudston in East Yorkshire where mosaics show Venus and Mercury,

The web which connected all these elements was the remarkable Roman road system. At first the roads were part of the military infra-structure, which allowed the rapid movement of troops and supplies to fight within the region against the Brigantes and then in Scotland. However, once built, the roads also served as excellent trading links which, associated with the navigable river systems, allowed the movement of goods throughout the country and the Empire.

Even though there is significant evidence for Roman occupation it was the native tribes and people who made up the majority of the population. Many lived as slaves or tenants of Roman landlords, or in their own small isolated farmsteads. Where such farmsteads have been excavated there is often little to show the influence of the Romans, except for some pottery. As well as farming there was also considerable lead production in the Pennines – indeed it has been suggested that it was the lead that was the principal objective of the Romans initially attacking the north.

YORK AND THE EMPERORS

Despite being a city on the furthest fringes of the Roman Empire, York had several documented visits by Roman emperors. The first emperor to visit was Septimus Severus between AD 209–211. His presence immediately increased the city's status, because with the emperor travelled all the machinery of government. The emperor had journeyed to York probably in order to quell the northern Caledonian tribes which had been attacking Hadrian's Wall. Septimus Severus held his Imperial Court in York until he died on 2 February 211. His remains were cremated, and then his ashes were shipped back to Rome. Severus's empress and his two co-emperor sons rushed back to Rome to secure their positions. Today there is still a reminder of Severus for a few miles from York there are three large mounds, called Severus Hills, and legend has it that this is where Severus's cremation took place and his ashes are buried.

One of Severus's two co-emperor sons, Caracalla, made a decision which helped to secure Eboracum's position as the second most important settlement in England, for he divided the previously single province of Britain into two. *Britannia Superior* was governed from London (Londinium) which controlled the south and west, whilst Eboracum was the provincial capital of *Britannia Inferior* (Lower Britain) which covered the north of England.

Almost one hundred years later, in AD 306, the Roman Emperor Constantius Chlorus was campaigning in the north and he too died in York. He was succeeded by his son Constantine, who was proclaimed emperor by the troops, probably on the site of the present Minster. Constantine went on to found Constantinople (now Istanbul) and was the first Roman emperor to convert to Christianity. He is now known as Constantine 'the Great'. Today Constantine's presence in the city is marked by a statue to him outside the Minster.

Constantius Chlorus's wife, and Constantine the Great's mother, was called Helena, and it was she who reputedly found the cross on which Christ was crucified. In later centuries there was a myth that she was the daughter of a local British chief. In fact, both Constantius and she were from Asia Minor, but the persistence of the myth in medieval times led to a number of churches around York being dedicated to St Helen. At the bottom of Stonegate, in the heart of York, stands the church of St Helen, one of the oldest in the city which may date back to Roman times.

FOOD AND TRADE

Roman food and diet consisted of local staple foods, supplemented by more exotic goods from overseas. The local foods included cereal based products, such as bread which could be made from wheat, barley and rye. Evidence for this was found in excavations in Coney Street where a Roman grain warehouse was discovered. The grain had become infested with grain beetles and to get rid of the problem the Romans covered the infested corn with a thick layer of clay. A second warehouse was then built on top, which was accidentally burnt down. As well as cereals, the Romans were great meat eaters. Beef was particularly popular, with mutton and pork also being eaten.

From further afield came crabs and herring, probably from the Yorkshire coast, and from overseas, olives, grapes, figs and wine. The olives, grapes and figs all have seeds which have been identified from archaeological excavations in York, whilst the wine was imported in distinctive wine jars, shards of which are commonly found. The bones of a dormouse have also been found – dormice were a delicacy and the preparation of stuffed dormice has been described in a cookery book written by the Roman cook Appicius.

As well as food, other items showed evidence of the wide trading networks, which can sometimes be pinpointed precisely. Jet items such as pendants and pins have been found in York and the only place in the Roman period that jet was found in England was Whitby, on the North Yorkshire coast. Pottery can be another excellent indicator of trade for different regions have distinctive styles of production or design. Samian ware, pottery with a beautiful reddish sheen, came from the Continent with central Gaul (modern day France) being a particularly important area.

Christianity in York

Christianity had been spreading across the Roman Empire ever since the missionary activities of the apostles and St Paul. It is not known when the first Christians arrived in Britain but there are numerous items with Christian inscriptions and symbols which have been found across England. Sometimes the nature of the evidence is unclear. One of the earliest pieces of evidence for Christianity was found in Manchester where a piece of pot had a Christian inscription on. However, as the pot had come from Spain this is flimsy proof of Christianity in England.

One certain Christian symbol has been found in York, the chi-rho monogram which is the first two letters of Christ's name in Greek. The symbol was found on a tile which was discovered during archaeological investigations of the Minster. A more problematic piece of evidence is the grave which contained a bone plaque with the words S(O)ROR AVE VIVAS IN DEO (O sister, hail! May you have life in God). The wording has been seen as Christian in sentiment but there was nothing else in the grave to indicate the person's religion. Thankfully we are on firmer ground with the final piece of evidence. In 314 Eborius, the bishop of York, was summoned by Constantine the Great to the Council of Arles to discuss Christianity in the Empire, along with the bishop of London and another bishop, probably from Lincoln. This is the sole reference to a bishop of York in the Roman period, but that he was bishop probably indicates a man who held sway over the province governed from York.

LATE ROMAN YORK

From the mid third century inscriptions mentioning York disappear. The last dateable reference to York occurs in AD 314. Why there are no later inscriptions is puzzling, especially as York itself was thriving. The initial fortress walls were of timber, but at some point between AD 275 and AD 325 the fortress walls overlooking the River Ouse were magnificently rebuilt in stone. The new stretch of wall was a symbol of Roman power and prestige. They may well have been ordered to be rebuilt by the Emperor Constantius Chlorus who was based in York and died in the city in AD 306. Amazingly one of the corners of this architectural achievement has survived. Today it is called the Mul-tangular Tower and it is located in the Museum Gardens.

Whilst York prospered, elsewhere in the Empire there was increasing dissension amongst the ruling elite. Rival emperors set up their own empires and for a time Britain, Spain, Gaul and Germany broke away from the central rule of Rome and became the 'Empire of the Gallic Provinces'. This separate Empire was short lived and lasted between AD 260 and 274

During the fourth century the central rule from Rome was once again weakened by usurpers starting civil wars within the Roman Empire and attacks from external enemies. In 367 there was the so-called 'Barbarian Conspiracy' during which raids were made from Scotland, Ireland and further afield across the North Sea. The attacks were initially defeated and thereafter the Roman forces attempted to seal the defences. Various measures were put in place, including a chain of signal forts to warn of impending attacks and raids. Such forts are known to exist at Filey, Ravenscar, Scarborough and possibly at Whitby.

However, as the fourth century progressed, sea-borne raids by northern peoples such as the Angles and Saxons became common and there is further evidence for measures to defend towns and cities. The

The Multangular Tower dating *c*. 300 from the old Roman fortress walls

evidence for increased defences in York is controversial and rests on a small tower known as the 'Anglian Tower', which is situated behind the Roman Multangular Tower in the Museum Gardens. The date of the Anglian Tower is debatable. When it was excavated the tower was thought to have been built later by the Anglo-Saxons – hence its name – but it is now believed to have been constructed during the late Roman period to defend the city.

At the end of the fourth century the Roman military presence in England had all but waned and across the country there are signs that there was a breakdown in authority. In York the buildings of the city were slowly becoming abandoned and neglected. Archaeological excavation has shown that in previously clean rooms rubbish was allowed to build up and the levels of cleanliness deteriorated.

One remarkable site shows the deterioration of an ordered system of government and how buildings changed their function through time. A large excavation was undertaken at a riverside site at Wellington Row which discovered a Roman warehouse. The warehouse had functioned well for a time and was kept clean. Then around *c.* AD 350 the warehouse became disused and within it people started to deposit small bronze coins. As well as the coins, a small pot was found and the skeleton of a lamb had been buried in a small pit nearby. The best guess as to what was happening is that it had become a sacred or votive site and that people threw in small coins for luck. Then even this site was covered by 'black earth' – a thick layer of earth which covers many Roman sites after they were abandoned.

Other features show that the glory that was once Roman York was fading. Minor streets were abandoned, some buildings were demolished, and debris accumulated in houses and the streets. The picture was the same nationally and one of the great symbols of Roman rule, the minting of coins, ceased in Britannia completely from *c.* 402. Coins are a means of trade and a measure of wealth and the cessation of production symbolises the collapse of the economy and the associated decline of Roman authority.

The twilight years of Roman rule in York, and Britannia as a whole, are difficult to gauge as there is practically no archaeological evidence in York during the fifth century. In the countryside the situation probably remained more or less the same, with villa owners still farming the rural landscape for a generation or so. Yet the military and economic infrastructure had gone and with few armed forces for protection Britannia was ripe for conquest.

New invaders were about to arrive on these shores: the Angles and the Saxons.

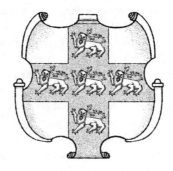

CHAPTER TWO

Anglo-Saxon and Viking York, 400–1066

The period following the departure of the Roman legionaries in the early fifth century is shrouded in darkness. There is only the faintest glimmer of evidence to illuminate what was happening. The most likely scenario is that there was a disintegration of the Roman infrastructure across England. Roman coins remained in circulation until about 400 but then stopped being used. Urban centres across England, including York, declined in importance and ceased to be the major economic centres that they had been under the Romans. Whilst a few people probably lived within York's walls, much of the city was covered in 'black earth', a puzzling depth of dark soil which is found in many English cities and dates to the century or so after the Romans left. York also disappears from the historical records – there is no mention of the city by name between AD 314 and 627 – over three hundred years.

The Anglo-Saxons arrive

From about AD 450 onwards wave upon wave of raiders and settlers from the Baltic region began to arrive in England. These people were the Angles and the Saxons – the Saxons deriving from what is now Saxony in northern Germany. East Yorkshire was one of the first regions in England to be settled by them, and evidence for their presence is shown by their graves. There are two possibilities as to why the Anglo-Saxons were in the region. The first is that it was a straightforward invasion by successive Anglo-Saxon warriors, who then brought over their families. The second theory is that the Romans used Anglo-Saxon troops as mercenaries or allies initially as protection from other enemies. This policy may have then backfired, with the Anglo-Saxons taking control of the land.

The Anglo-Saxons brought with them new ideas and today their influence can still be seen in the landscape, mostly obviously through place names. There are thousands of Anglo-Saxon place names scattered across England. Elements within place names show that the places were given their names by the Anglo-Saxons. The place name elements of '-ton', '-ham', and -'ley' are all elements of Anglo-Saxon and roughly mean village, hamlet and clearing in a forest. Further research has revealed that a rough chronology can be established. Places with the element -ing- within them, such as Birmingham in the Midlands or Islington in London, or Heslington just outside York are very early Anglo-Saxon names and relate to a particular people, so Heslington means 'the ton belonging to the people (ing) of Hesl'. Around York there are other Anglo-Saxon place names such as Clifton, Shipton and Stockton.

The study of place names is a fascinating one, though fraught with difficulties. It is often unknown when a place was given a name (the first recorded examples may be centuries later) and settlements sometimes disappeared or moved from their original locations.

Burials are another key source of evidence for the Anglo-Saxons. The greatest concentration of burials and finds is in the Yorkshire Wolds between York and the North Sea coast. Burials are a key indicator of these new peoples for they buried in a distinctive way, by cremating their dead and putting the ashes into urns. It is often not realised how much energy (both human and in terms of timber) is needed to cremate a body and it is much easier to dig a hole and place a body into it. The largest Anglo-Saxon cemetery in the north is at Sancton on the Yorkshire Wolds which probably contains thousands of cremated burials.

The actual number of settlers has caused some debate. It is possible a relatively few Anglo-Saxon settlers seized control of the most powerful positions of society. The alternative is that there was a full scale migration of Anglo-Saxons from across the North Sea. The large number of Sancton burials point to a large immigration – or would do if many other large Anglo-Saxon cemeteries existed. Other cemeteries and burials are known but few have more than fifty burials or cremations.

EVIDENCE FOR ANGLO-SAXONS IN YORK

Whilst the new Anglo-Saxon population is visible in Yorkshire, it is difficult to see any evidence for the earliest Anglo-Saxons in York at all. There are a small number of cremation burials which have been on The Mount and in Heworth – a suburb of York – but little else. However, with the arrival of the new settlers the name of the city became corrupted, from the Roman 'Eboracum' to the Anglo-Saxon 'Eoforwic'. The Anglo-Saxon name has two elements: *eofor* meaning 'wild boar' and *wic* meaning farm, trading centre or small settlement.

As the Anglo-Saxon presence became more established York once again became an important centre. Whilst few people might have lived in the city compared to Roman times, the city became a symbol of power for the local kings.

ANGLO-SAXON KINGDOMS:
BERNICIA, DEIRA AND NORTHUMBRIA

Gradually Anglo-Saxon kingdoms emerge from the historical shadows. At first, following the collapse of Roman control, new, or possibly pre-Roman, power blocks emerged. They formed a patchwork of evocative sounding kingdoms across the north of England and southern Scotland, with names such as Bernicia, Deira, Elmet, Rheged, Strathclyde and Gododdin. To the south of York lay the kingdoms of Lindsey (roughly modern day Lincolnshire) and Mercia located in the Midlands. Within each of these kingdoms there were smaller groupings, for example there was the sub-kingdom of Hatfield between Elmet and Lindsey. The exact details of their boundaries remain unknown, though the names of some kings have survived, such as King Mynyddod the Wealthy who reigned in Edinburgh.

Some of these separate kingdoms kept their own identities for several centuries, the most important of which in the north-east of England were Bernicia and Deira. Deira probably covered the area that is now East Yorkshire, bounded by the North Sea coast to the east, the River Humber to the south, York on the western boundary and the North

York Moors to the north. One possible derivation of the name Deira is from the British word for oak (*daru* or *deru*) which is also probably the derivation of the name of the River Derwent. If the river and the kingdom are connected, then the Deirans are the people of the River Derwent. Bernicia, which means 'land of the mountain passes', stretched from its borders with Deira in the south northwards into the region which is now the Scottish borders.

Although Bernicia and Deira were the most powerful kingdoms, other smaller kingdoms also existed, such as Elmet. Defining the boundaries of Elmet is problematic, but there are many clues. Two still exist as place names in the form of Sherburn in Elmet and Barwick in Elmet which place the kingdom to the west and south-west of York.

Whilst Deira had Anglo-Saxon kings, Elmet had native British rulers. Gradually the Anglo-Saxon influence from the east coast kingdoms of Deira and Bernicia prevailed in the north and the native British identity gradually receded. Around AD 600 a Bernician Anglo-Saxon king emerged who began to conquer other kingdoms, either through battle or by subjecting the lesser kings to pay tribute to him. His name was Aethelfrith and at the fullest extent of his power his kingdom stretched from present-day Edinburgh to the Midlands. With lesser kings and kingdoms under him, Aethelfrith had become the first 'over king' of the north.

As certain kings and kingdoms grew in power at the expense of lesser kingdoms, a great northern powerblock began to form which was known as Northumbria. The first recorded use of the term 'Northumbria' occurs in the early eighth century. Initially this was simply a description of the land and people who lived north of the Humber, but as kings came to rule most of northern England the kingdom of Northumbria became a reality.

Paganism and Christianity

During the Roman period Christianity had spread through England and in York there was a bishop of York. Following the collapse of Roman rule Christianity ceased in large parts of England. By AD 500 there were only small pockets of Christian life based in remote monasteries in Wales and Scotland. In Ireland the great patron saint of that country, St Patrick, was converting the people to Christianity. St Patrick and his successors were so successful that one hundred years later Christian missionaries from Ireland started to evangelise and convert the peoples of Scotland and northern England once again to Christianity.

In Yorkshire, however, the paganism of the Anglo-Saxons dominated religious life. The details of pagan practice remain obscure because the later Christian writers wanted to praise Christians, not describe pagan practices. However, from clues and partial descriptions, paganism seems to be based around the agricultural and yearly calendar. Charms and sacrifices (though probably not human in England) were also an important part of the ritual. On a more personal level amulets, spells and particular plants were considered to protect the wearer. Pagan Anglo-Saxons did not have the alphabet that is used today, but wrote in runes. Each rune is made up of a series of straight strokes that can be easily carved into rock, stone or bone. There are odd indications that paganism also had a hierarchy of priests, though these would probably have been purely local. There is no evidence of a national, or international, formal pagan organisation. This was in direct contrast with Christianity with the pope in Rome who had influence internationally.

King Edwin and the Conversion to Christianity

Just after 600 King Aethelfrith reigned across the north of England and his success resulted in his opponents fleeing southwards. One of Aethelfrith's enemies was Edwin, king of Deira. Edwin fled to the court of Raedwald, king of the East Angles, whose powerbase was in East Anglia. Raedwald is a fascinating figure, as powerful in the south as Aethelfrith was in the north. Evidence of Raedwald's power came to light in 1939 when excavations at Sutton Hoo, near Ipswich, uncovered a magnificent treasure. Although it cannot be proved, the grave is assumed to be that of Raedwald. Today the Sutton Hoo treasure can be seen at the British Museum. Raedwald was a nominal Christian, though it is known that he set up two altars, one to the Christian god and another to the pagan gods. To many pagans Christ was another god to worship and, like Raedwald, many must have hedged their religious bets by praying to both Christ and pagan gods.

Raedwald collected an army and marched north and in the ensuing battle Aethelfrith died. Edwin returned to the north, taking Aethelfrith's place as 'over-king' of the region. King Edwin was still a pagan, but he married the Christian Kentish princess Aethelburh. One of the conditions of the marriage was that she brought her own priest, Paulinus into the court. Paulinus, who was an Italian bishop, instructed Edwin in Christian beliefs, but Edwin was still undecided and called together his chief men. One of them gave a graphic example of the difference between how he saw Christianity and paganism. Paganism he said was like sitting in a large hall, warmed by a fire, whilst outside wintry storms and rains are raging. Suddenly a sparrow flies through a window into the warm hall and out of the opposite window. For a moment the sparrow is warm, but then flies out once again into uncertainty. The new Christian religion, however, gives certainty about what happens after death, therefore he argued that Christianity should be followed.

Other chief men gave their opinions and as a result of the debate Coifi, the chief pagan priest, declared his own beliefs 'worthless'. In a great act of defiance against pagan beliefs he rode to the shrine in the East Yorkshire village of Goodmanham and profaned it by throwing in a spear. This act settled the dispute in favour of Christianity. Today Goodmanham is a charming village with an impressive church, though with no tangible reminder of the ground-breaking events that took place there.

Through a combination of the chief men renouncing paganism and Paulinus's teaching King Edwin agreed to be converted to Christianity. The importance of converting the king was that all his subjects were expected to follow his example. In effect the conversion of a king at a stroke converted thousands more. How sound this conversion really was caused some concern amongst missionaries of the time, as many converts reverted back to their pagan beliefs.

King Edwin was the most powerful king in the north and he set about enhancing his status and reputation by building a church in York. The church was initially built of wood so that he could be quickly baptised and then after his baptism he built a second, larger, church of stone. It was in this church that some of Edwin's children were buried after they had died in infancy. The church was dedicated to St Peter – a dedication which survives to this day. As well as having a church, York also became the Diocese of York and Paulinus became the bishop of York.

Edwin's power was short lived and in 633 he was killed at the battle of Hatfield, only six years after being converted, by the pagan king of Mercia, Penda. Paulinus fled south with Edwin's widowed queen and children, and York was once again ruled by a pagan king. One Christian priest, James the Deacon, remained at St Peter's. Following Edwin's death the kingdom of Northumbria divided into its two main constituent parts, the kingdoms of Deira and, to the north, Bernicia.

CELTIC AND ROMAN CHRISTIAN MISSIONARIES

Paulinus was part of the missionary programme from Rome. The first missionaries from Rome were led by St Augustine who arrived in Kent in 597. However, in the north there were Christian missionaries following different Celtic Christian practices coming from Ireland, who founded the Scottish island monastery at Iona. These monks followed the teachings of St Columba, and from Iona their influence spread through Scotland. One significant convert was that of Oswald, who in 634 became king of Bernicia.

With his new power Oswald began actively promoting the Irish or Celtic form of Christianity throughout the north. He established a monastery on Lindisfarne which became not only the centre of the diocese of Northumbria, but also the base of missionary activity throughout the north of England. Across the bay from Lindisfarne was Oswald's own palace at Bamburgh.

In 642 Oswald was killed during a battle with the pagan king of Mercia, Penda. Oswald became revered as a saint and martyr, and at the place of his death on the battlefield many miracles were recorded. Oswald's successor was his brother, Oswiu whose fortunes in war against Penda fluctuated but in the end he successfully defeated and killed Penda in battle. One of the results of Oswiu's success was that the Irish church gained a still greater presence in the north of England.

However, the Irish Christian missionaries were coming into increasing conflict with the missionaries from Rome in the south of England. The differences between the two groups ranged from their appearance to their beliefs. The Roman clergy had what is today thought of as the traditional tonsure, with their hair being cut away at the crown of the head. The Celtic tonsure cut the hair away from the front half of the head following a line running from ear to ear. A more serious point of contention between the churches was that Easter was calculated differently. In extreme cases a king, following Roman practice, would still be fasting and facing hunger through Lent, whilst for his queen, following Celtic practice, had celebrated Easter. As she was no longer fasting she could eat sumptuous feasts.

The debates and arguments between the two versions of Christianity raged with each gaining the upper hand at different periods of time depending on the connections with the ruling king. The decisive moment occurred during the Synod of Whitby in 664 which was held at St Hild's monastery at Whitby on the North Yorkshire coast. The events were written down by the Anglo-Saxon monk and historian Bede. King Oswiu of Northumbria acted as the final arbiter over the debates. The crucial argument occurred over the method of computing Easter: whether to follow practice of the Roman missionaries (and therefore St Peter), or the Celtic method (and therefore the founding father of Celtic Christianity St Columba).

In a final speech Oswiu argued that it was St Peter who held the keys to heaven and therefore the Roman method was adopted. The religious consequences were profound. Although not immediate, Roman missionaries steadily gained influence in the north of England. Gradually the Roman church not only gained dominance but also lands and wealth as it was becoming the norm for Christian kings and nobles to give lands, possessions and even relatives to the care of the church.

THE ARCHBISHOPRIC OF YORK 735

Since the departure of Paulinus from York in 633 the church in York largely disappears from the records and it was the bishop of Northumbria, based in Lindisfarne, who ruled the church in York. Then, for reasons now unknown, the centre of the diocese was moved from

Lindisfarne to York, probably soon after the Synod of Whitby in 664. For the next seventy years there are occasional references, the longest being about the restoration of the church which was undertaken by Bishop Wilfrid of Hexham in 669–71. Bishop Wilfrid arrived to find the roof leaking, unglazed windows and 'birds [which] flew in and out, building their nests, whilst the neglected walls were disgusting to behold owing to all the filth caused by the rain and birds'. Wilfrid's repairs left a transformed building, with the whitewashed walls being 'whiter than snow', along with a proper altar and ornaments.

Then in 735, after seventy years, York was suddenly promoted to become the seat of the archbishopric, who was in charge of the other bishops and their dioceses of the north. This was a remarkable reversal of fortune for the church at York, and it is disappointing to discover that the reasons for the sudden promotion in status are now totally obscure.

The creation of an archbishopric of York was what Gregory the Great had originally wanted when he sent St Augustine to England to convert the Anglo-Saxons 138 years earlier in 597. Gregory's idea was to create an archbishopric in each of the two greatest Roman cities in England: London and York. However, Gregory's information was out of date and when Augustine arrived in England the Anglo-Saxon king of Kent ruled from Canterbury, not London. Therefore Canterbury became the seat of the southern archbishop. In the north the centre of ecclesiastical power lay at Lindisfarne, until the unexplained promotion of York. The archbishop of York now had his seat (*cathedra*) in the cathedral at York.

The church of St Peter's is today often referred to as the 'Minster'. A minster was an Anglo-Saxon 'mission station' whereby groups of clergy were based, who then cared for the Christians of the diocese. This was very different from the later system which emerged, whereby individual clergy cared for the church and souls of a parish. The minster system was a much more dynamic system, but also meant that apart from at the minster itself, there was no permanent Christian presence in the towns and villages of the diocese. Many churches, large and small, have kept their 'minster' names, from cathedrals such as Beverley Minster, to large parish churches – Howden Minster – to magnificent churches – Westminster Abbey in London – to the tiny, ancient and charming church of St Gregory's Minster near Pickering.

The Venerable Bede (673–735) and the Artistic Achievements of Northumbria

One of the great advantages of Christianity was that it is, unlike paganism, a religion based on the Word, the Book (the Bible) and writing. This in turn meant that events were written down – a key consideration for kings who wanted to be portrayed as glorious, and even more anxious for their heroic deeds to be immortalised. To have not only God, but also the written word on one's side was a powerful reason for conversion. The Anglo-Saxon monasteries were the centres of learning in the Anglo-Saxon world and each had a writing room called a *scriptorium* and a library. Some of the most famous monasteries and nunneries were those in Northumbria.

The largest of the Northumbrian monasteries were located on the coast or tidal inlets. The southernmost in Northumbria was at Whitby, and then moving northwards there were the monasteries of Hartlepool, Jarrow, Monkwearmouth and Lindisfarne. At one time historians thought that the monasteries were deliberately placed in the wilderness to remove monks from the temptations of the world. However, recently it has been recognised that far from being in out of the way places, these monasteries were on key sea-bourne trading routes to Europe, as well as guarding the rivers leading into Northumbria. Traders crossing the North Sea or sailing along the coast would have had to pass these churches. The monasteries and nunneries were often ruled by abbots and abbesses of royal blood, enhancing not only their status, but also the royal dynasties grip on the kingdom.

The monasteries, with their royal associations and trading links, were the centres of the written word, and the great artistic achievements of the age. It was the 'Golden Age' of Anglo-Saxon art. The monasteries in Northumbria were particularly famous for their intellectual learning and magnificent manuscripts, including the *Lindisfarne Gospels* and the *Codex Amiantinus*, both large and magnificent volumes. The *Lindisfarne Gospels*, which were created at the monastery on Lindisfarne, can today be seen in the British Museum. The *Codex Amiantinus* is now in Italy, but this one book alone weighs the equivalent of a Great Dane dog. The number of animal skins required to make such books was enormous. For the three great Bibles produced at the Jarrow monastery over 1,500 skins were required, which in turn shows the resources which the wealthy monasteries had at their disposal.

In York, however, the evidence of this great Golden Age is, today, non-existent. It is known that the Anglo-Saxon library of the Minster was a renowned one, but the books have long since been destroyed. There are a few fragments of metalwork from archaeological excavations which show intricate patterns on belt buckles and other pieces, but to all intents and purposes the evidence of Anglo-Saxon artistic achievement from York has been lost.

Some light has been shed on the situation in York by the Venerable Bede. Bede was the greatest English scholar of the age and was a monk in the monastery at Jarrow on the River Tyne. His work encompassed a huge range of interests from works about religion, to the lives of saints, to the meticulous work about systems of time. Indeed Bede has been credited with starting the practice of counting years from the birth of Christ, thereby creating the term AD, or *Anno Domini* (The Year of Our Lord). His most famous work was *The History of the English People* which describes the history of Christianity in the British Isles during the early Anglo-Saxon period. There is nothing like it anywhere else in Europe and without it the history of the times would be much darker. There are also many incidental details including the fact that a young cowherd, Caedmon, sang in Anglo-Saxon about the Creation in the monastery at Whitby – the first known English poet.

Bede however, was not working in isolation. There was an outpouring of great art and manuscripts and sculpture from the increasing wealthy Northumbrian monasteries. It was during this period that St Cuthbert lived, first at Lindisfarne, and then as a hermit on the Farne Islands. After his death miracles occurred at his tomb and he became the most famous saint in the north. Although vandalised at the Reformation enough of Cuthbert's tomb survives to show the incredible workmanship of the period. Onto his wooden coffin were carved the figures of angels and Christ's apostles and Cuthbert himself wore a fine gold cross inlaid with jewels. The objects in the tomb show how far the cultural and trading contacts of the monasteries could be: Cuthbert's comb was made from ivory from Africa, a shell within his cross came from the Red Sea or Indian Ocean and other items look to Ireland, Gaul, Italy, Egypt and the Middle East for their inspiration.

By the end of his life Bede was becoming more pessimistic about the fate of the church in Northumbria, because the golden years of Christianity seemed to be fading. Bede died in 735 and from then on the historical record becomes much dimmer without his description of events.

Alcuin of York (c. 732–804)

Alcuin was educated at York Minster, and then became its teacher and librarian. He was considered the greatest teacher in Europe and his reputation was made in 782 when he became the master of the court school of Charlemagne – the phenomenally powerful ruler whose empire covered modern day France and Germany. It is an indication of the reputation of English learning that Alcuin should have been chosen as master. During his lifetime he was amongst the foremost theologians and grammarians in Europe and was passionately interested in the arts, language and the written word, and it is widely believed that he invented the question mark. Alcuin returned several times to England and Northumbria, but in his last years he settled in the monastery of Tours in France and became its abbot.

Despite living on the Continent, Alcuin never forgot his native city of York and wrote many letters to the community in the Minster. He also composed a long poem 'On the Saints of the Church of York' which mentions various archbishops but is vague about life in York itself. Alcuin does, however give a description of the new Minster, which was built after its predecessor was burnt to the ground in 741.

> A lofty building, raised on solid piers
> Supporting rounded arches, and within
> Fine panelling and windows made it bright,
> A lovely sight...

This building has long since been destroyed and this short description is all that remains to what once must have been one of the finest churches in England.

The Coppergate Helmet

The Coppergate Anglo-Saxon helmet is the single greatest Anglo-Saxon find ever discovered in York and ranks alongside the greatest in England. It was found completely by accident as the major excavation in Coppergate was in its closing stages. A mechanical digger was operating in an area thought to be clear of archaeology when suddenly the digger's bucket struck an object in the ground. On closer inspection the driver realised he had found something unusual and called over the archaeologists working nearby. It turned out to be a magnificent Anglo-Saxon helmet which has been dated to between 750 and

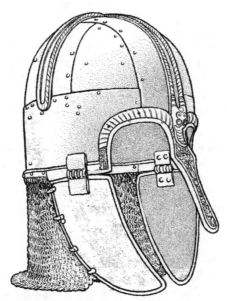

The magnificent Anglo-Saxon Coppergate helmet

775 AD. Over a thousand years later it came very close to being destroyed as the Victorians built the base of a large chimney just centimetres above it.

The helmet is of the highest standard of workmanship and has a chain mail neck guard made of about 2000 rings. The helmet is made of iron but has brass inlay and decoration, either as an intricate interlace of swirling beasts or as an inscription running across the helmet in strips. The inscription is in a slightly abbreviated and corrupt form of Latin and infuriatingly can be translated in different ways, though one way is 'In the name of our Lord Jesus Christ and of the Spirit of God, let us offer up Oshere to All Saints, Amen'. The reference to All Saints may refer to the church of All Saints Pavement which lies close by and Oshere could well have been a founder or patron of the church. Oshere is otherwise unknown, but if he owned the helmet then he was a powerful figure in York who could have been influential on a regional scale at the same time that Alcuin was in York.

The Vikings

From Alcuin's vantage point on the Continent he could see a looming threat to Britain and in 797 he wrote 'The greatest danger overhangs this island ... A pagan people habitually make pirate raids upon our shore ...'. Alcuin was right to be concerned. Four years earlier in 793 the *Anglo-Saxon Chronicle* had recorded

> In this year dire portents appeared over Northumbria and sorely frightened the people. They consisted of immense whirlwinds and flames of lightning, and fiery dragons were seen flying in the air. A great famine immediately followed these signs and a little after in the same year, on June 8th, the ravages of the heathen men miserably destroyed God's church on Lindisfarne with plunder and slaughter.

One wishes there had been fiery dragons – in reality it was probably a spectacular display of the Northern Lights, which are rarely seen so far south. However, the heathen men were real enough and the year 793 marks the start of the devastating raids by the Vikings on the country. The Vikings in their long ships attacked the wealthy monastery at

Lindisfarne and looted its treasures. The raid was a harbinger of centuries of turmoil to England as the Vikings raided, looted and eventually settled.

The Vikings have sustained over the centuries a fearsome reputation as blood-thirsty warriors out to sack and loot the lands they attacked. The notoriety was well deserved, though it was not the total picture. As well as England they attacked across Europe, into modern day France and the Low Countries. In England the raids became more and more frequent with huge flotillas of ships sailing across the North Sea to attack the relatively undefended coasts.

The term Viking is a loose one to describe the peoples of Scandinavia and Denmark. The root of the word 'Vik' may come from the Norwegian word meaning 'to wander' or 'travel'. The term Viking however, has the great advantage of conjuring up a particular image of a helmeted warrior with a large sword and shield (incidentally, the Vikings did not wear horned helmets – wearing a horned helmet in battle would be difficult). The first Viking raiders did not follow a single king and the Viking groups often fought amongst themselves. Different groups settled in different locations and the Norwegian Vikings settled along the north west coast of England whilst the Danish Vikings favoured Yorkshire and York. As the Vikings settled and merged into the local population academics tend to use the term 'Anglo-Scandinavian' to describe the people who lived in the areas settled by Vikings.

THE EFFECT OF THE VIKINGS

The Vikings had a long history of raiding England through the centuries and they were fearsome warriors against whom the peoples of England rarely had an effective defence. The initial shock of the attack on Lindisfarne in 793 led the way to other strikes on the vulnerable monasteries along the exposed coasts. In 794 the rich Anglo-Saxon monasteries of Monkwearmouth and Jarrow were plundered with other monasteries being stormed over the following decades.

Yet, what effect did the Viking attacks have? The events which were recorded with most horror by contemporaries were the Viking assaults on monasteries with the Vikings looting them of their precious holy objects and causing extensive damage. Such raids have often been cited as the reason why the large and famous Anglo-Saxon monasteries disappear from the historical record during the Viking period. However, the reasons for their collapse may be more subtle. Rather than their destruction being caused by burning and looting (for they could be rebuilt and re-provisioned) it may be that the estates from which they gained their wealth were seized by the new Viking lords. Without the income from their lands the monasteries folded.

THE VIKINGS STAY IN ENGLAND

Following the initial lightning Viking raids over the following centuries Viking tactics changed and evolved. The year 850 marked one such change in tactics. Before that date they had raided England and then returned home, but for the first time the Vikings 'over-wintered' in a base on the Isle of Thanet near London. With a secure base in England the Vikings no longer had to make the perilous North Sea crossing and could strike rapidly at any time of the year. In 866 Viking tactics changed again. This time, rather than attacking with bands of raiding warriors, the Vikings formed a great army which stayed as a unit in East Anglia over the winter.

The Vikings were highly opportunistic in when they attacked and, therefore, in 866 they took full advantage of a civil war between two claimants to the Northumbrian throne. Marching northwards from East Anglia they crossed the Humber and they captured York. York was an incredible prize. It was a royal city at the heart of the kingdom of Northumbria, with a long trading tradition across the North Sea.

The rival Northumbrian claimants to the throne were slow to unite to attack Vikings. When they did counter-attack the results were disastrous as the Vikings decimated the Northumbrian forces. Both rival kings were killed. The remaining survivors made peace with the Vikings, who imposed a puppet king to rule Northumbria. Other kingdoms also began to fall to the Vikings. East Anglia was conquered in 870 and Mercia in 874.

Even though the Vikings held York, it was a Viking held city surrounded by lands still held by Anglo-Saxons. However, this was about to change. In 875 the *Anglo-Saxon Chronicle* recorded that the Viking army had split in half. Half went further north and fought for control of lands either side of the present-day Scottish border (the kingdoms of Bernicia and Strathclyde region). Although initially successful, Viking control of this area was soon overthrown in the late eighth century by local 'Saxon' nobility based in their stronghold at Bamburgh.

Between the rulers at Bamburgh and the Midland kingdom of Mercia lay the Viking territory of Yorkshire. In 876 the other half of the Viking army, which was led by Healfdene 'shared out the land of the Northumbrians and they proceeded to plough and support themselves'. Healfdene's men carved up the territory and became the owners of estates, villages and farms. The Viking warrior elite now had a permanent presence in Yorkshire: they were here to stay, not just raid. York became the focal point around which the Viking kingdom grew. By 880 the ancient Anglo-Saxon kingdom of Northumbria had fragmented into two with the Saxon rulers in the north at Bamburgh and the Viking kingdom of York in the southern portion.

THE ANGLO-SAXON COUNTER-ATTACK

The political and military situation in the rest of England was highly fluid. The greatest kingdom was that of Wessex in the south. King Alfred the Great (871–899) was its most powerful king but even he was taken by surprise by Viking tactics and had to flee into the marshes and take refuge at Athelney – where legend states, he burnt the cakes. Whether true or not, the legend reveals the humiliating position Alfred had been reduced to. Alfred regrouped his forces and successfully drove the Vikings from his kingdom of Wessex.

Alfred's son, Edward the Elder, continued to defeat the Vikings and regained control of the Midland kingdom of Mercia, and Edward's son, and Alfred's grandson, Athelstan achieved even greater success. In 927 the *Anglo-Saxon Chronicle* recorded simply that Athelstan 'succeeded to the kingdom of the Northumbrians'. Athelstan marched north to claim his territory and overlordship of the North. Athelstan gained control over York and the northern rulers – Ealdred of Bamburgh, Constantine of the Scots and Owain of Strathclyde – all proclaimed Athelstan's superiority. It is highly likely however, that they did so through gritted teeth as these regions were fiercely independent and the only reason for their agreement was Athelstan's overwhelming military force. To counter Athelstan's superiority an alliance was formed between Olaf Guthfrithson, king of Dublin and Constantine of the Scots. This alliance posed a powerful threat to Athelstan, but he further stamped his authority on the region by a devastating military victory. The site of the battle was called by the Anglo-Saxon chronicler 'Brunanburh' and although the precise location of the site is now lost, it was probably near the River Ribble in Lancashire.

Eric Bloodaxe

Ever since Anglo-Saxon times York had been the most populous, and therefore wealthy, city of the north. After the death of Athelstan in 940 the king of Dublin Olaf Guthfrithson seized York and the surrounding territory. The link between York and Dublin is still in evidence by the name of a small alley called 'Dublin Stones' leading from the River Ouse to North Street. Although it was first written down many centuries later it is tempting to see it as a remnant of trading between York and Dublin when they were both ruled by the kings of Dublin. For the next fifteen years York was ruled by a succession of Viking kings, though it is difficult to piece together the exact details of the chronology of their reigns.

It was during this time that one of the most colourful rulers of York emerged: Eric Bloodaxe. The Vikings often gave their rulers evocative names such as Harald Bluetooth, Ivarr the Boneless or Harald Fine Hair, but Eric Bloodaxe conjures up a truly fearsome warrior. He was a former king in Norway and his name was given to him for his bloodthirsty ways. It is unfortunate that the only written evidence for his rule in York comes from sagas, and only copies from later centuries have survived. The sagas described Eric as 'Hot-headed, harsh, unfriendly and silent ... he rules York under the helmet of his terror'. One saga involved the famous Viking poet Egil Skallagrimsson who was shipwrecked at the mouth of the Humber and made his way to York, even though it was ruled by his enemy, Bloodaxe. Bloodaxe only agreed to his freedom if Egil composed a poem in praise of him, which Egil did and recited the next morning. Bloodaxe was delighted and ordered his release. Bloodaxe ruled twice, once for about a year until he was ousted from York, and then from 953–4. He was killed travelling north in a battle on Stainmore – a wild and bleak moor in County Durham.

From Eric Bloodaxe's death the political situation in York, and the north generally, is confused, but in the south other kings, notably Edgar and then Athelred 'the Unready', were crowned as kings of England. Although a long reign, Athelred's was disastrous. The term 'Unready' by which we know him today is a corruption of the Anglo-Saxon word *unraed* which has a variety of appropriate meanings: 'ill-advised' or 'no-counsel', which is a double pun as Athelred own name means 'good counsel'.

During Athelred's reign new Viking attacks swept through the country, first led by King Swein of Denmark, and then his son, Cnut. It was Cnut (who is known to many by the English spelling of Canute), who attempted unsuccessfully to turn the tide back. However, the moral of the story is now largely forgotten. Cnut's courtiers had suggested that Cnut's power was greater than God's, so to disprove their ideas Cnut showed them that God had ultimate control.

Viking York

Throughout the Anglo-Saxon and Viking eras York was the second largest city in England, after London. It had a population of about 9,000 people and was a port of international significance. There are references of merchants from Denmark and Frisia and in the work describing the life of St Oswald, who was archbishop of York between 971 and 992, York is described as a 'city beyond expression, and enriched with the treasures of merchants, who come from all parts, but above all from the Danish people'.

An insight into life of the city was uncovered by the archaeological excavations at Coppergate. The archaeologists discovered Viking houses with walls made of wooden planks, boundary fences made of wattle and cess pits, which were holes used as toilets in the backyards of the houses. The cess pits were important discoveries as they revealed

The intricate carving on part of a copper Viking scabbard

the diet of the Vikings, which included beef, mutton and pork, sea-food such as eels and herring, and fruit and vegetables – apples, berries, pears, carrots and beans. There were also some unusual finds rarely recovered from excavations such as a knitted sock, as well as commonly found leather shoes and dyed pieces of cloth. There was also evidence of widespread trading contacts. These included a cap made of silk, millstones from Germany, amber from the coast of Denmark and a conch shell which came from either the Red Sea or the Indian Ocean.

As a city York had a large number of churches, most of which were in private ownership. Powerful nobles and rich merchants founded churches for their own spiritual needs, but also to increase their own riches, because people paid to christen their children, be married and be buried. These churches tended to be small, though often made of stone which made them stand out from the normal wooden and thatch houses. The Minster was the great exception. Although the site is not known for definite (it is probably under the park next to the present day Minster) and no images exist, it towered above all other buildings of the city.

The Earldom of Northumbria

In the south of England there had been more of less constant warfare between the Anglo-Saxon kings and the Vikings, but in 1016 the

Viking King Cnut became undisputed king. However, he still had to subdue a restless country and he promoted a system of government which relied on powerful magnates to control the regions. These individuals were called 'earls'. Within York the earl of Nortumbria had his principal residence in 'Earlsburgh', an area which today equates with the Museum Gardens. The earl of Northumbria at the time was Utred, who, in the political chaos, had been waging his own private war against the earl of Mercia.

With Cnut's succession a major priority was to bring the north back under the king's control. Cnut marched north and captured York.

MASSACRE AT WIGHILL

Between York and Tadcaster stands the small settlement of Wighill. Today it is chiefly visited by tourists (if it is visited at all) to look in the church, but in 1016 the name was known throughout England as the place where Earl Uhtred of Northumbria was murdered. Even an earl of Uhtred's power and wealth was not a match for Cnut and a peace treaty was to be agreed at Wighill. (The Anglo-Saxon name of 'Wiheal' cannot be located with certainty, but it is presumed to be at Wighill.) Earl Utred and his household entered the hall where Cnut had based himself, and as was the Anglo-Saxon custom the men had left their weapons outside as a gesture of peace. Unfortunately this was a grave mistake, as an arch enemy of Uhtred's, Thurband and his men – with Cnut's agreement – emerged from their hiding place and massacred Uhtred and all his party.

Cnut's position was now even more secure as king, but the massacre set off a chain reaction between the families of the key noblemen, with Uthred's son Ealdred killing Thurband, and Thurband's son Carl killing Ealdred. Ealdred's grandson then killed Carl's son and grandsons in 1073–4. The spiral of violence only seems to have stopped with the imposition of the new Norman rule in Yorkshire and Northumbria after 1069.

EARL SIWARD

To secure his control of Northumbria King Cnut appointed Siward as earl of Northumbria. Today Earl Siward is known principally as a minor character in Shakespeare's *Macbeth*. In York he is remembered for two reasons. The first is that there is an Iron Age burial mound by the University of York library called 'Siward's Howe', though the reason for this name is now forgotten. The second is that in 1055 Siward died and was buried in his minster 'which he himself and built and consecrated in the name of God and Olaf'. St Olave (a corruption of the Norwegian saint's name Olaf) still stands as one of the most historic churches in York in Marygate, off Bootham.

Siward was a powerful earl and expanded Northumbria to the west, to take in Cumbria which included the area of the Lake District. Siward also had considerable involvement with the politics of Scotland. When Macbeth came to power following the murder of Duncan, Duncan's young sons, Malcolm and Donald, and his brother fled into exile – into Earl Siward's protection. The princes were in fact distantly related to Siward through marriage so they were his kin as well as guests.

Thereafter Siward helped the refugees to try to reconquer their kingdom. An invasion was launched in 1046, which failed. Between 1050 and 1053 the king of Scots, Macbeth, went on pilgrimage to Rome, but on his return Siward and the exiles launched a successful invasion in 1054 at a battle at Dunsinane – the site of which is now lost. With this victory, Duncan's son Malcolm became king. (Macbeth actually survived the battle and fled, but three years later was killed in another battle.) Siward's success against Macbeth was short lived, for although he was loaded with riches for his help in defeating Macbeth, his eldest son and nephew had died in the fighting. Siward died soon after in 1055 and was buried in his new foundation of St Olaf's in York.

YORK AND THE END OF THE VIKING ERA

In 1055, following the death of Earl Siward, Tostig was made ruler of Northumbria. Tostig had a Danish mother but his father was Godwin, who had been the powerful earl of Wessex. Godwin's other children had a strong grip on the rest of the country. Godwin's daughter, Edith, was married to the king, Edward the Confessor. But it was Godwin's eldest son who held the greatest earldom of all – Wessex. The only other family in the kingdom with any considerable power was that of Leofric, earl of Mercia. (It was Leofric's wife, Godiva, who made her famous nude ride through the streets of Coventry in an effort to reduce the taxes on the citizens imposed by her husband.)

Tostig's task of holding a fractious Northumbria was made more difficult by the king of Scotland, Malcolm III, marching south in 1058. The raid resulted in destruction, followed by a truce. The occasion of the agreeing of the truce may have been the only time that the English king, Edward the Confessor, journeyed north to York.

Tostig was a man on the move and despite – or perhaps because of – the turbulence of Northumbrian politics he was not often in the region. In 1061 Tostig went on pilgrimage to Rome, and in his absence Malcolm again ravaged Northumbria. When Tostig returned to England he didn't pursue Malcolm, but instead fought for his brother Harold, earl of Wessex, against the Welsh in 1063–4. In the meantime Tostig's enemies were gathering their forces.

In the autumn of 1065 Tostig's Northumbrian enemies gathered and marched south. They captured Tostig's household and seized his arsenal and treasury. As so often in his rule Tostig was not in Northumbria. Instead he was hunting with his brother Harold. News soon reached Tostig of the revolt and he and his family fled to Flanders. In place of Tostig the rebels chose Morcar, the grandson of Leofric, Earl of Mercia. However, Tostig was about to return.

1066

King Edward the Confessor died on 5 January 1066 and his death completely changed the political situation in England. There were numerous contenders to the throne, but the obvious choice was Harold, earl of Wessex. Harold was duly crowned at Westminster. As Harold was Tostig's brother there was a strong possibility of a frosty reception for Harold in York, but his visit in the spring seems to have eased tensions.

Gradually Northumbria was calming down. The appointment of the inexperienced Earl Morcar had meant that the local nobility had a freer reign than before, and with Tostig gone the dynastic links with Wessex and the south had weakened. All would have been well except that Tostig wanted his power back and was determined to seize it any cost.

Sailing from Flanders he attacked ports along the south and east coast and in Scotland he joined forces with Harald Hardrada, king of Norway.

VIKING VICTORY AND LOSS: YORK AND STAMFORD BRIDGE

The joint forces of Harald Hardrada and Tostig sailed down from Scotland, up the Humber estuary and along the River Ouse. Their target was York. The fleet landed at Riccall, about ten miles south of York. A hastily collected defending force was mobilised by the Earl Morcar, with his brother Edwin, the earl of Mercia. Why they chose to face the Vikings just outside York, rather than from its defended walls, is unknown, but battle was fought at Gate Fulford on 20 September 1066, within sight of the city itself. The battle is thought to have been a short, sharp bloody skirmish and the native forces under Edwin were severely beaten. Tostig – this time with Harald Hardrada – once again was in possession of the city. However, from the security of York's defences, Tostig's and Harald's forces withdrew to Stamford Bridge.

Why Stamford Bridge was chosen has never been fully explained, though one reason is that the Viking forces moved from York to await important hostages which would ensure the good behaviour of the local inhabitants. It proved to be a tactical mistake, because the Viking forces not only left behind the security of a fortified city they also moved further away from their ships at Riccall. The army of Hardrada and Tostig therefore left themselves militarily exposed. It was to be a matter of days before once again York changed hands.

Elsewhere in England the politics had been unfolding since Edward's death. Although Harold was king, other claimants to the throne had emerged. None was more dangerous than Duke William of Normandy. It was the threat from William that Harold had taken most seriously and for the whole of the summer the two sides had been preparing for war. William had collected his army and had hurriedly built or requisitioned ships to carry his troops across the English Channel. Harold too called out the Anglo-Saxon militia, called the *fyrd*, but as the summer of 1066 dragged on and there was still no sight of William the possibility of invasion lessened by the day. William's delay had been caused by contrary winds in the Channel, but they changed and William set sail.

Harold however had other things on his mind, because he had marched north to counter the threat of his brother Tostig and Harald Hardrada. The resulting battle was at Stamford Bridge. The speed of Harold's march from the south had taken Hardrada and Tostig completely by surprise. A key point of the battle occurred when a single fearsome Viking warrior held the bridge across the river, and so the English army could not cross. The situation was resolved when a crafty English soldier got into a barrel and paddled downstream until he got under the bridge and then forcefully jabbed a spear between the legs of the Viking warrior. The bridge was thus cleared and Harold and his army were able to cross. Harold won a spectacular, if hard fought, victory. Both Tostig and Hardrada lay dead on the battlefield. The remnants of the Viking army, including Hardrada's son Olaf, and the earl of Orkney, retreated to Riccall. The force had arrived in several hundred ships. They sailed home in just twenty-four.

A few weeks later the history of England was to be changed by the arrival of Duke William of Normandy and Harold's defeat and death at the battle of Hastings. The Viking era had ended forever.

CHAPTER THREE

Norman and Plantagenet York, 1066–1272

The Norman Conquest: The Arrival of the Conquerors

Ever since the Viking capture of York, York and Yorkshire had had its own kings and rulers. Whilst a king or ruler could capture the city, they were dependent on local support from the nobles of Yorkshire and Northumbria. Therefore leaders were sometimes 'invited' into York. If the people of York and Northumbria did not like a new ruler, then he could be forced out. Earl Tostig was one such ruler who was forced to flee overseas after being removed by a powerful alliance of local nobles.

However, William the Conqueror (1066-87) was about to impose both his own will, and his own nobles, onto the people of Yorkshire. William had defeated and killed the last Anglo-Saxon king of England, King Harold, at the battle of Hastings in 1066. Initially William concentrated upon securing the south of England and the north was relatively calm. Morcar, the new earl of Northumbria, and his brother Edwin, earl of Mercia had submitted to William soon after Hastings and in return for their submission they were allowed to keep their lands.

CASTLES AND REBELLION

In 1068 William the Conqueror journeyed northwards to take personal control of York and the whole of Northumbria. The citizens of York and Northumbria had never liked the imposition of rule by a southern king, and the fact that William and much of his army was from Normandy and other areas of the Continent probably made the situation even worse. William was not a monarch who dealt delicately with local situations and like many other cities and towns throughout England the Conqueror imposed his will by force. The standard method was to build a castle.

The notion of a castle was a new one in England (though one or two had previously existed on the Welsh borders). The standard design of a Norman castle was 'motte and bailey' which can be defined as a high mound (the motte) with a fortified courtyard below (the bailey). On top of the mound was a further structure – the keep. The castle was designed for maximum strength for a lord and his garrison to withstand attack by a much larger force.

The first signs of William's desire to subjugate the people of York was the building of a castle in the city in 1068 and the replacement of Earl Morcar, earl of Northumbria, by the powerful Norman lord, Robert de Commines. Commines quickly became hated by the Northumbrian nobility and was killed at Durham.

The local York population also rose up and besieged the castle. To add to the threat, one of the royal Anglo-Saxon princes, Eadgar, was preparing to march with a force from Scotland. William lost no time in once again marching north. The speed of his advance caught the rebels completely by surprise and William raised the siege of the castle. It was at this point that the second castle was built in 1069 for additional strength and security.

Today both castles survive, though in very different states. The most important throughout York's history is called York Castle, of which the most impressive single element which still stands today is Clifford's Tower. York Castle developed into the centre of county administration and was one of the most important seats of the sheriff of Yorkshire. The second castle which lies just across the river is Baile Hill. Today all that remains is a large mound covered with trees. It quickly fell out of use and in the Tudor period in the sixteenth century it was used for archery practice. However, even though the relative importance of the castles is not now in doubt, there is considerable dispute about which was built first. Owing to the fact that York Castle became incredibly important and strategically significant, lying as it does between the River Ouse and the River Foss, it is generally assumed that this was the first to be built, though the truth may yet surprise historians. The importance that William gave to the city is shown by the fact that there were two castles – the only other city in England to have two castles was London. The reason that they span the river is so that a chain could be thrown across to stop Viking ships attacking the centre of the city. Initially the buildings in the castle were made of wood and Clifford's Tower was only rebuilt in stone during the thirteenth century.

Not surprisingly, the people of York and the Northumbrians deeply resented the imposition of the castles. The scale of the castle building programme is such that the two castles 'laid waste' one of the seven Anglo-Saxon shires – or administrative units – which covered the whole city. The threat from the local residents and other claimants to William's throne came together when King Swein of Denmark landed with a large fleet of ships in the Humber. Local and foreign nobles joined together to form a powerful coalition against the Conqueror. They marched on York and attacked the castles. As part of the Norman garrison's resistance, the defenders set fire to the houses surrounding the castles. The fire became uncontrollable and proceeded to burn a large part of the city. This did not stop the attackers, the castles were over-run, and the garrison decimated. On 20 September 1069 York was once again in Viking hands.

THE HARRYING OF THE NORTH

Even though York was in Viking hands, the motivation of King Swein of Denmark was to attack, loot and retreat, rather than a serious attempt to conquer the north. The Danes returned to their ships in the Humber estuary. William, who had been campaigning in the south, rapidly marched north and made a treaty with King Swein, who then sailed away.

This was to be William's third and final invasion of Yorkshire and this time he left nothing to chance. It was autumn and he devastated the Yorkshire countryside in a military operation now called the Harrying of the North. The scale of the Harrying is now unknown, but it was certainly considered by near contemporaries a devastating campaign even by the standards of the day. On William the Conqueror's deathbed the chronicler Orderic Vitalis wrote down what William thought about the Harrying of the North:

> I [William] treated the native inhabitants of the kingdom with unreasonable severity, cruelly oppressed high and low, unjustly disinherited many, and caused the death of thousands by starvation and war, especially in Yorkshire ... I descended on the English of the north like a raging lion, and ordered that their homes and crops and furnishings should be burnt at once and their great flocks and herds of cattle and sheep slaughtered everywhere ... alas! [I] was the cruel murderer of many thousands, both young and old of this fair people.

William's campaign effectively meant the end of all opposition in Yorkshire.

As if to prove the point William the Conqueror held a formal crown wearing ceremony in York at Christmas 1069. Such ceremonies took place three times a year – Christmas, Easter and Whitsun – and were a huge and impressive gathering of the important churchmen and nobles of the kingdom. The assemblies were a combination of decision making, pronouncements and royal image making, with all the most important churchmen and nobles of the kingdom being present. The attendance of so many rich and important people together with their retinues must have given a much needed temporary boost to the local merchants and shopkeepers of York.

Following the collapse of the rebellion in 1069, there was no further major upsurge of local anger, though the resident Anglo-Scandinavian population must have been smarting from the actions of their new lords.

THE NORMAN PRESENCE IN YORK

Once William and his army had left York after the last rebellion, the remaining Normans might well have felt isolated. However, as part of the Conquest the city began to experience a huge range of changes. Firstly the castles were rebuilt. The most important, later called York Castle, dominated the entrance to the city by river. A further element of the defences of the city was the damming of the River Foss and the resulting creation of the King's Fishpool. The Fishpool was a huge lake, the effects of which lasted over 850 years until it silted up and was reclaimed as building land. In the later Middle Ages the fishpool was also called the Marsh. It formed part of the defences of York and is the

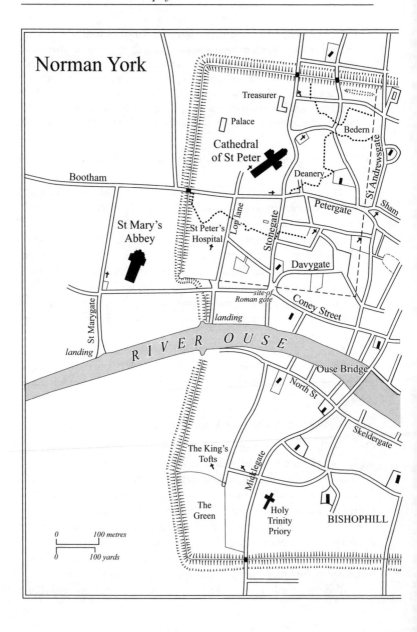

Norman York

Treasurer

Palace

Bedern

Cathedral
of St Peter

Bootham

Deanery

St Andrewsgate

Petergate

Sham

St Mary's
Abbey

St Peter's
Hospital

Loop lane

Stonegate

Davygate

site of
Roman gate

Coney Street

landing

RIVER OUSE

St Marygate

landing

Ouse Bridge

North St

Skeldergate

The King's
Tofts

Micklegate

The
Green

Holy
Trinity
Priory

BISHOPHILL

0   100 metres

0   100 yards

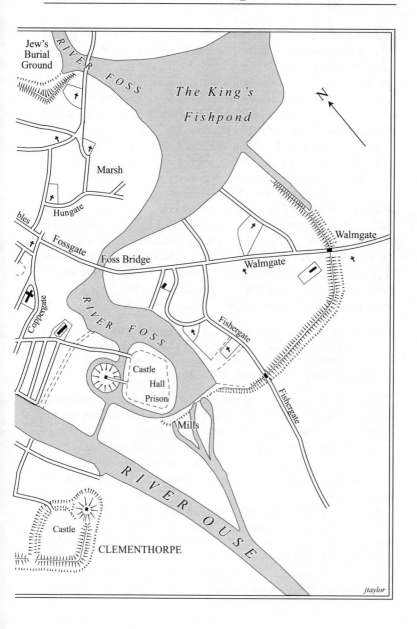

Jew's Burial Ground

RIVER FOSS

The King's Fishpond

N

Marsh

Hungate

bles

Fossgate

Foss Bridge

Walmgate

Walmgate

Coppergate

RIVER FOSS

Fishergate

Castle
Hall
Prison

Fishergate

Mills

RIVER OUSE

Castle

CLEMENTHORPE

jtaylor

reason why the city walls do not totally encircle the city. The fishpool gave its name to an area of the city which is reflected in the medieval names of two churches St John's in the Marsh and St Saviour's in the Marsh. The effects of the fishpool lasted until the early twentieth century, but today all that remains of this once impenetrable barrier are a few road names, in particular Foss Islands Road which is a reminder of the islands which formed in the Fishpool.

Whilst the castles and the fishpool formed a crescent of change at one end of the city, huge new building projects were being undertaken at the other end. Rather than military projects, the other building programmes involved churches. The largest single project was the building of the new Norman Minster. The Anglo-Saxon archbishop of York, Ealdred, had died in 1069, and was replaced by an energetic new Norman archbishop, Thomas, from the Norman monastery at Bayeux. The churches in Normandy were dynamic and reforming and Thomas of Bayeux was very much of that tradition. The situation that he discovered in York was appalling. A York chronicler, Hugh the Chanter, wrote that when Thomas arrived

> he found everything laid to waste as a result of enemy action. Of the seven canons (priests) he found three in the burnt and ruined church. The rest were either dead or driven away by fear and devastation. Thomas reroofed and to the best of his ability rebuilt the church ...

Thomas set about rebuilding the Minster, but rather than restoring what had been, he built an entirely new church in front of the Anglo-Saxon Minster. It was a propaganda move and statement of power. Although the sequence of events has not yet been determined, it is easy to imagine the political statement that the huge new stone Norman Minster made as it was erected in front of the ruined Anglo-Saxon one.

As well as the new cathedral which towered over the city at one end and the castles at the other end, there were other major building projects completed before 1100. In Micklegate the church of Holy Trinity became a monastery. The house was an 'alien' monastery, which meant that it was controlled from outside England, and was one of the family of monasteries dependent upon Marmoutier in France.

Parish churches too were being rebuilt in the new Norman Romanesque architectural style. The masons who would have worked on
larger projects, also brought their craftsmanship to the smaller churches.
At St Denys's church the arch over the doorway has zig-zag and foliate
patterns whilst St Nicholas's tower doorway even has a carving of a
dragon.

THE FOUNDING OF ST MARY'S ABBEY

Before the Norman Conquest all the Anglo-Saxon monasteries in the
north had disappeared. The great Anglo-Saxon monasteries at Whitby,
Jarrow, Monkwearmouth and Lindisfarne had perished because of a
combination of the Viking attacks and then seizure of monastic land
which starved them of financial support. By 1066 the northernmost
monastery was at Burton upon Trent in the Midlands, one hundred
miles from York.

Within a few years of the Conquest monasteries once again began to
be founded in Yorkshire. The first was at Selby when a monk named
Benedict escaped from his own monastery in Normandy and, carrying
the precious relic of St Germanus's finger under the skin of his arm,
made his way to Selby and founded the abbey there.

Apart from the abbey at Selby, the story of major monastic revival in
the north started in the west country monastery at Evesham. There
three monks gathered together: Aldwin, Elwy and Reinfrid. It is
probable that Reinfrid was a soldier in William the Conqueror's army
and so had first hand knowledge of the north. The three of them set out
deliberately to find the ancient Anglo-Saxon monastic sites mentioned
in the writings of Bede. They first settled at Jarrow. The most interesting of the three monks from the viewpoint of the history of York is
Reinfrid. After Jarrow he moved to Whitby where the derelict monastic site, originally founded by Abbess Hild, was reinhabited by the
monks. Reinfrid was then succeeded as abbot by Stephen. However,
the fear of attack became too much for the monks and so they moved
to the wilds of the Yorkshire Moors where they settled at Lastingham.
Stephen and a group of other monks then moved once again – this time
to found St Mary's Abbey in York. They were given a small plot of land
beside St Olave's church and then over the centuries the monastery of

St Mary's Abbey became the largest, and one of the wealthiest abbeys in the north of England.

The Domesday Book 1086

As the city, and England in general, was settling down to the rule of William the Conqueror, he instigated one of the greatest administrative feats of English history. At Christmas 1085 William the Conqueror ordered a survey of land ownership of his nobles throughout England. The result was the remarkable Domesday Book. (Domesday is pronounced 'Dooms-day'.) Domesday records every city, town, village and settlement from Yorkshire southwards in considerable detail, though, the information it records can be fragmentary and confusing. Even so it is a beacon of light upon the country and is a rich source for historians.

Information on the city of York is given in considerable detail. The city was divided up into seven shires, one of which belonged to the archbishop, and another had been requisitioned for the castles. The boundaries of these shires have now been lost but it shows there was a degree of internal organisation within the Anglo-Saxon city. Entries record landlords and tenants: 'Hamelin has one messuage in the town moat, and Waldin has one message of Einulf and one messuage of Alwin'. A number of important Normans feature in the city, such as Hugh, son of Baldric, Robert Malet and Odo the crossbowman. The Domesday Book also gives a precise figure for the number of houses in five of the seven shires: 1,418 dwellings. From this, allowing for five people per dwelling, it is estimated that York, the second biggest city in the kingdom, had an estimated population of just over 9,000 people – about the same as a small market town today.

LIFE IN YORK

Following the devastation caused by the conquest and rebellion the physical fabric of much of the city had to be rebuilt or repaired. The building of the two castles by the Normans had resulted in the destruction of one of the seven Anglo-Saxon shires. A fire had also swept away the houses around the castles. At the other end of the city was the ruined Anglo-Saxon Minster. Whilst these examples were described by the records, there was likely to have been widespread destruction of houses and shops throughout the city.

The Normans implemented huge schemes which changed the face of York forever. York must have been a hive of industry with building stone arriving by river and then been taken through town. There were also all the traditional trades continuing, such as leather working and comb making, but also new trades were responding to the fashions of the times, such as the spur makers, who congregated in the street named after them: Spurriergate.

People were usually given surnames either associated with where they had come from, or their trade. Soon people came to York from nearby, such as Robert of Clifton (now a suburb of York), whilst Paulinus of Leeds came from that city. Occasionally an international connection can be made, for example Hugh of Rouen. Surnames connected with trades included Thomas the goldsmith and Robert the dyer.

The physical fabric that the Normans found was a mixture of Viking, Anglo-Saxon and Roman. Even though over six hundred years had past since the Roman era, and the city had undergone wave after wave of attacks and new settlers, there were a surprising number of Roman buildings and structures still standing. The walls around the fortress, and especially on two sides of the Minster, were still strong enough to form a reasonable defence and a basis on which the later medieval walls were to be built. We know that one Roman building at least at the very end of the Viking era or early Norman era was still standing because it was dismantled and then stone by stone was used to build the church tower of Bishophill Junior. (The 'Junior' element was used because another church was called Bishophill 'Senior'. This latter church was flattened in the 1960s – only a graveyard remains.) Recent excavations on a portion of the Roman walls near the Multangular Tower – a fine Roman part of the walls which survives to this day – shows that a portion of the Roman walls was used as part of the new hospital of St Leonards.

Stone structures were however, the exception to the rule. Wooden buildings dominated the city. Even the impregnable castles were built out of wood (they were only rebuilt out of stone a hundred and fifty years after the Norman Conquest). Fire was a constant hazard. The deliberate firing of the houses around the castles in 1069 has already been mentioned, but accidental fire was a constant threat. Occasionally the owners of buildings were so fearful of fire that charters – the legal documents by which property changed hands – had clauses relating to fire included in them. When Roger de Wynchon rented a house to Roger the cook and his wife Eva a clause stated that 'if the buildings are burnt down by fire or are destroyed or deteriorate for any other reason' the house should be rebuilt to the value of twenty marks. As Roger was a cook, and therefore probably had a larger than average oven in his house, this was a sensible clause to include. At one time it was thought that York was devastated by fire in 1137 but a recent theory is that in the past the Latin word for 'consecration' (*consecrata*) has been misread as conflagration, (*conflagrata*). This in turn means that the theory relates to the archbishop of York consecrating various churches in 1137 – no doubt with colourful processions and as a big religious occasion – rather than a fire destroying the city.

All too few fragments of life and customs are recorded about the city. The chronicler William of Newbrugh wrote that some boys built 'childish houses [and] yoked mice in little wagons...'. One can imagine

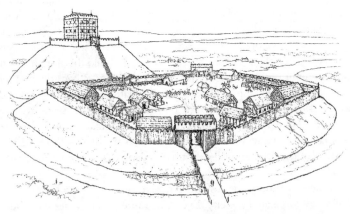

How York castle may have looked in the twelfth century

the mice pulling the little wagons behind them as the children watched in delight. At one point young boys threw stones at the hearse of Archbishop Gerard, but only because he had been accused of witchcraft.

Religion played a major part in people's lives. The constant danger of being tempted into sin by the devil and the threat of hell meant that people were very wary of the wiles and snares of the devil. Demons and hell were regularly depicted in stained glass windows, wall paintings and sculpture. In the crypt of the Minster there is a stone called the 'Doom Stone' which is a large carving of devils forcing souls through the jaws of Hell and into the fiery furnace below.

Some exceptional people could actual see devils and their snares for the unwary. A man called Ketell who lived in the village of Farnham had this power. Some of the devils he saw were 'large, robust and crafty', whilst others 'were small and contemptible, impotent in strength and dull in understanding'. Some he saw throwing stones in the way of travellers to make them trip, and once he saw a covered wagon escorted by laughing devils. On asking the devils what was happening the devils replied: 'We are conducting to the place of punishment the sinful souls deceived and ensnared by us and they are bewailing while we are laughing at them', whereupon Ketell banished the devils and released the souls.

The pattern of life can be described with broad brush strokes. Meals would have been eaten at midday and in the evening. Different days of the week had different traditions. Fish was eaten on a Friday and markets were held on Sundays. The church authorities disliked the timing of the markets and frequently attempted to ban Sunday trading. They were only successful in 1322, over two hundred years after the custom probably started.

Just to make matters confusing there were four recognised start dates for the year. Christmas was probably most common during the late eleventh and early twelfth centuries, but 25 March (the Annunciation or Lady Day) became more common in the later medieval centuries. Other dates included 1 January (the Feast of the Circumcision) and Easter. Then, as now, the calendar of the church ran from Advent to Advent, starting on 30 November, with its associated fixed and moveable feast days. Some dates were fixed, such as Christmas, but others depended upon Easter, the calculation of which was determined by the phases of the moon.

HYGIENE AND HOSPITALS

Hygiene during the Middle Ages was not a priority and by today's standards the conditions were dirty and unpleasant. Archaeological excavations have revealed that large amounts of debris built up in the streets, in backyards and even in people's houses. There were different trends at different times and in the Roman period and then the later medieval period after *c.* 1300 conditions improved, but between these dates people had little regard for environmental cleanliness.

One of the great medical concerns of the age was that of leprosy. Although rare occurrences of leprosy were known in Anglo-Saxon England, for some reason after the Norman Conquest leprosy became much more widespread, and with it the fear of the disease. Its contagious nature resulted in lepers becoming segregated from society by being put into leper houses. Most towns and cities in England had leper hospitals and York was no exception. Leper hospitals were located outside the walls of the cities and York's leper house was St Nicholas's Hospital, outside Walmgate Bar. The leper hospitals were enclosed communities usually run by religious men and had accommodation, chapel and graveyard.

There were other hospitals too, the largest of which was St Leonard's Hospital. In its hey-day it was the largest hospital in the north of England, housing 206 patients, though in 1399 there were 232 people. The hospital was a combination of a place for the sick to be healed, old age care and an orphanage and many people stayed there for years. Although the internal arrangements are unknown for St Leonards, at other large hospitals in England it was not unusual in times of plague for several people to share the same bed. Although St Leonards was swept away during the sixteenth century Reformation, some of its buildings can still be seen. The vaulted undercroft and ruined chapel above still remains next to the City Library. The area that the hospital covered was a large one and there are remains of the hospital a distance away under the present theatre in St Leonards Place.

ST MARY'S ABBEY AND THE FOUNDATION OF FOUNTAIN ABBEY 1132

The monks who settled in York and founded St Mary's Abbey after the Norman Conquest were Benedictine monks so called because the monks lived by a set of rules formulated by St Benedict. For hundreds of years the Benedictine Rule was the only rule, but on the Continent groups of monks reacted to what they considered to be the lax lifestyle of the Benedictine monasteries and set up their own stricter rules for monastic living. The most important group was the Cistercian monks, so called because the movement originated in Citeaux, now in modern day France. The Cistercians were a stricter order than the Benedictines and lived a severe and devout life. There was also an important administrative difference between the Cistercians and the Benedictine orders – all the Cistercian monasteries across Europe were organised from the monastery at Citeaux, whereas the Benedictine monasteries were all individually run without a formal hierarchy. The organisation abilities of the Cistercian monasteries resulted in a powerful and wealthy religious body which spread across Europe.

The Cistercians were particularly active in Yorkshire. The first group to arrive stopped off at St Mary's Abbey on their way northwards, and then went onto found Rievaulx Abbey. However, their stay in St Mary's resulted in serious dissension. On one side were the monks who wanted to follow the stricter life of the Cistercians, who were led by Prior Richard, who was second in command. On the other side were the followers of the elderly leader at St Mary's, Abbot Geoffrey, who wanted to continue as they had always traditionally lived.

The day 17 October 1132 has been described as 'one of the most dramatic in Yorkshire history' for on that day, the archbishop of York, Thurstan, and supporters of both sides visited the Abbey. The arguments became heated, so much so that the monks supporting Abbot Geoffrey shouted 'Grab them, seize them'. Prior Richard and his followers only escaped by clinging to the archbishop for protection. After this event there was no turning back and Prior Richard and his followers journeyed to a site near Ripon and founded Fountains Abbey. A short time later the community joined the Cistercian Order. Other

Cistercian communities settled in Yorkshire and founded what were to become some of the greatest of the medieval monasteries in England: Jervaulx, Meaux, Bylands and Kirkstall.

Within a hundred years of William the Conqueror's victory at Hastings, religious practice in Yorkshire had been revolutionised. Monasteries once again flourished and their presence tied Yorkshire into a vast European network. The Cisterian Order alone had 328 monasteries across Europe in 1154. This network not only encouraged monks to communicate with each other, but also encouraged education, learning and trade.

The Anarchy 1135–1154

The name 'The Anarchy' is the later term given to the period of warfare between the death of King Henry I in 1135 and the succession of Henry I's grandson, Henry II, in 1154. The conflict arose following the death of Henry I's only son, Prince William, in a shipwreck. Henry had no other legitimate sons and so the succession passed to his daughter, Matilda. Matilda had been married at the age of fourteen to the elderly Holy Roman Emperor who ruled what is now western Germany and so she became an empress in her own right. After a few years her husband died and she married again, this time to Geoffrey, Count of Anjou, who ruled a territory which bordered Normandy.

Following Henry's death there was a brief vacuum of power and instead of Matilda travelling triumphantly to London to be crowned, her cousin Stephen, Count of Blois quickly sailed across the English Channel and was crowned king. Not surprisingly Matilda bitterly resented this, and fought Stephen for the crown.

During the Anarchy Yorkshire was an important strategic stronghold for Stephen because the king of Scots was an ally of Matilda's. Stephen was therefore anxious to appoint people loyal to his cause in Yorkshire and it resulted in him creating the title of 'Earl of York' for William Aumale, the powerful lord of Holderness. William was the only person in history to hold this post as it was abolished when Stephen's successor, Henry II (1154–89), came to the throne. Thereafter there was no noble title associated with York until the creation of the title of duke of York two centuries later.

Stephen's support in York and Yorkshire remained firm and twice the armies of the Scottish king came south and both times were defeated. The second time was in 1149, but fortunately the sight of Stephen's army resulted in the Scottish army's rapid retreat. The first time, however, the march south by the Scots had resulted in one of the bloodiest battles of the Anarchy – the battle of the Standard in 1138.

THE BATTLE OF THE STANDARD 1138

In 1138 the Scottish army, led by King David, reached within thirty miles of York. The nobles of Yorkshire and people of York rallied together and led by the Thurstan, archbishop of York, they marched out to meet the Scots. The two armies met at a site three miles north of Northallerton and fought a battle known as the Battle of the Standard. The standard in question was that of St Cuthbert of Durham and it was carried to the site in a cart. The use of a saint's standard to give spiritual protection and fortitude to an army was a common practice on the Continent, but was a rarity in English battles, and why it happened in this case is unclear. The English army was relatively well trained and organised, and easily defeated the brave if ill-disciplined Scots.

St William – York's Own Saint 1154

In the middle years of the twelfth century York became the centre of an international power struggle within the church. The trigger for the dispute was the election of a new archbishop of York after the death of Archbishop Thurstan. The clerics of the Minster put forward their own candidate, William Fitzherbert, the treasurer of the Minster. He also had excellent royal connections, as his father, Herbert, had been chamberlain to Henry I and his mother was half-sister to King Stephen. With the backing of the clerics in the Minster, and King Stephen, William was elected archbishop in 1143.

However, his election was quickly disputed by the massively

William of York – York's own saint

influential Cistercian monk Bernard of Clairvaux and the Cistercian abbots of such Yorkshire monasteries as Fountains Abbey and Rievaulx. The dispute became known to the pope, Eugenius III, who unsurprisingly agreed with the opinion of the Cistercians, as he himself was a Cistercian monk. William was forced out of office and the Cistercian abbot, Henry Murdac, was installed as the new archbishop of York.

William never surrendered his claim and toured southern Europe proclaiming his right to be archbishop. His travels took him, amongst other Mediterranean lands, to Sicily. There is a possible indication of this visit in a small beautifully carved statue in the Minster of a Virgin and Child. The style of the clothes and the way the Virgin and Child are sitting are more like examples found in Sicily than in Yorkshire and it may be that William either brought it back with him, or a sculptor travelled back to York with William's entourage on his return.

In 1153 William's luck suddenly changed when his three key opponents, Henry Murdac, Bernard of Clairvaux and Pope Eugenius, all died. This left the way clear for William to re-establish himself as archbishop and he made a triumphal return to the city through throngs of cheering people. At this point a potential tragedy occurred, for the wooden Ouse Bridge collapsed under the weight of people and many were thrown into the river. Fortunately, and some said miraculously, no one was drowned and the incident became William's greatest miracle. A couple of centuries after the event the scene was depicted in stained glass, which can still be seen in York Minster as part of the St William window about his life.

William suddenly died after holding a mass on the 8 June 1154. The speed of his death led to suspicions of poisoning, and although nothing was ever proved, the story was widely believed. By the end of the century a cult had started based on William and a shrine had been built in the Minster. In 1226-7 William was finally made a saint when the pope canonised him. On 9 January 1284 the body of St William was moved from the nave to the more prestigious position behind the High Altar. At the event was King Edward I (1272-1307), his wife Queen Eleanor, ten bishops and numerous magnates.

During the changes at the Reformation in the sixteenth century St William's shrine was destroyed, but some stone fragments from the shrine were found in the eighteenth century which show beautifully carved stonework. Some images of the shrine and its surroundings have also survived in the St William Window. Around the shrine itself were offerings to St William from people who had been cured by him. Many of these were made of wax and depicted the nature of the cure – so a wax leg is shown, a wax arm or a head. This practice was common at all shrines and there is a report of Edward I leaving a wax statue of a falcon at a shrine as a grateful offering for restoring his falcon to health.

There were also political reasons for York having its own saint, and a key reason was the 'primacy' dispute. The primacy dispute was a long running and contentious dispute between the two English arch-bishoprics of York and Canterbury who argued who had ultimate power within England. The two archbishops were often personally involved and on one occasion when a cardinal visited England the archbishop of York attempted to sit on his right hand side, which was the prestigious and senior side, with the result that 'the servants of the lord archbishop of Canterbury rushed upon him and threw him to the ground, kicked him with their feet and tore his hood'. At the sign of such aggression the cardinal ran away and the meeting never took place.

Immediately after William died in 1154 there was little attempt to create a cult, but then in 1170 one of the most momentous events in English history took place – the murder of Thomas Becket, archbishop of Canterbury. The death of an archbishop by the servants of King Henry II had an impact not only in England but across Europe and a major cult quickly started around Becket's tomb in Canterbury Cathedral. An important saint of international stature gave Canterbury considerable religious and political influence. It may well have been the case that to match Canterbury's new saint the Minster authorities needed to promote their own, and so William's cult was started and grew. The competition between Thomas Becket and William was an unequal one. Whilst Becket was known throughout Europe, William at best was only a saint of regional importance. A firm decision about whether Canterbury or York had primacy over the other was never made, but increasingly it was recognised that Canterbury had the superior power. Today Canterbury Cathedral is the senior Anglican archbishopric in the British Isles.

THE YOUNG KING'S REVOLT 1173–4

The second great conflict of the twelfth century after The Anarchy was the Young King's Revolt which occurred in 1173–4. It is called the Young King's Revolt because King Henry II's son, who had been crowned as king and was also called Henry, revolted against his father. The main fighting in the north took place in the Scottish border region, but during the revolt the citizens of York were plotting on behalf of the Young King. Various citizens had smuggled weapons into the city and then distributed them to supporters of the Young King. The plot was discovered by agents loyal to King Henry II and the smugglers were fined heavily for their disloyalty.

The Jews and the Jewish Massacre 1190

The first Jewish community came to England in the decades following the Norman Conquest of 1066 and settled in London. The earliest references to a Jewish community in York occur in the 1170s. The Jewish community in York was never numerous and recent estimates put the number at around two hundred. However, by loaning money to Yorkshire landowners the community became prosperous and a few men, such as Aaron of York, became so wealthy that he was a financier to the Crown.

The Jewish community was not segregated from the population and they had a concentration of property in the heart of York along Coney Street and Jubbergate. It was in Coney Street that the community had its synagogue near St Martin's Church. It is unknown what the relations between the Jews and other Christian residents were like in the early years, but gradually tensions increased as the loan repayments became onerous to local landowners.

In 1190 the tensions erupted and the Jewish population of the city were attacked by a frenzied Christian mob. The order of events is known in some detail. Two eminent Jews, Benedict of York and Josce, attended Richard I's coronation at Westminster. Whilst there they were beaten by a mob and violence against Jews quickly spread through other towns and cities of England. The Jewish communities in Norwich, King's Lynn, Stamford, Bury St Edmunds and Lincoln were all attacked. However, the worst atrocity occurred in York. The mob attacked Jewish houses and the Jews fled to the safety of the royal motte and bailey castle, making a refuge for themselves in the high motte. Their peril was not over for the mob laid siege to the castle from the bailey below. The sheriff should have dispersed the mob, but he was out of York. The siege continued for almost a week – what might have started as a frenzied, spur-of-the-moment attack had developed into a serious and prolonged blockade. The Christian attackers even had time to build large siege engines to batter the walls of the motte. With the mob closing in, Rabbi Yomtob of Joigny suggested the Jews take their own lives and it was Josce who set the example by cutting the throats of his wife and sons. By daybreak there were few Jews left alive. The remaining survivors were tricked out of the castle with the promise of safe passage, only to be killed by the mob.

Anti-semitism played a part, but the large debt that the Christians owed to the Jews was a major factor in the passion of the attack. Local nobles who had borrowed money from the Jews were unable or unwilling to pay it back. After the siege had ended the conspirators then destroyed the documents recording their debt. They marched to the Minster where the Jewish bonds were stored and set fire to them in the middle of the nave. One of the main ringleaders was a local minor nobleman called Richard Malbysse, whose surname can be translated as 'evil beast'. The family surname still survives as the village place name Acaster Malbis, just outside York.

Law and order was re-established and the ringleaders fled the country with many men from York being heavily fined. The Jewish community re-established itself in York and there are many references to them after the massacre. Today there is a permanent reminder of the horrific events of 1190 as a plaque, written in Hebrew, has been erected at the bottom of the steps of Clifford's Tower.

York Governs Itself: 1212

Throughout the twelfth century York had been governed by the sheriff of Yorkshire, whose base was in York Castle. The citizens of York had bought charters from previous kings, such as Henry II and Richard, which gave them certain freedoms, but these charters still assumed the sheriff would have control over appointments and the city. The sheriff therefore controlled the administration of the city, and many wealthy citizens resented his power. As well as their increasing wealth, the citizens also began to act as a cohesive body and they formed a powerful group within York.

Their chance for self-rule came during King John's reign. King John (1199-1216), through disastrous and costly military campaigns, was in desperate financial straits, and one way to raise money was to allow citizens of towns to buy liberties from him so that they could govern themselves. King John's charter of 1212 to the citizens of York for the first time allowed them not only to organise and pay the city's annual payment to the Crown directly, but also to appoint a mayor, without any interference from the sheriff. In 1217 Hugh Selby was appointed as York's first ever mayor. His family thereafter dominated city politics for the next seventy years. Hugh was mayor six times, his son John seven times and his grandson Nicholas four times. In the following reign Henry III granted two more charters which resulted in the sheriff losing all power in the city.

However, even with the charters the mayor and corporation did not have authority over the whole city because there were many areas outside of the corporation's control. The largest area was the lands owned by the churches, whether by the Minster or the monasteries, but other areas outside the corporation's control included the castle which was under the auspices of the sheriff of Yorkshire. These areas, called 'liberties', remained a thorn in the side of the city authorities especially when criminals took refuge in them. The boundaries were also a potential area for contention and a long running battle took place between the citizens of York and St Mary's Abbey over their respective rights in Bootham. Another dispute occurred between the citizens and the Minster authorities, when the mayor took it upon himself to arrest and hang a woman called Annabella, even though she was a tenant living within the Liberty of the Minster.

RELIGION IN YORK *c.* 1220

By 1200 there was an established pattern of religious provision in York. A large number of about forty parish churches were distributed across the city. Many of these had originally been built by wealthy citizens both for their own use, but also in order to produce an income from the money generated from baptisms, weddings and funerals. By 1200 many of these private churches were being given into the hands of the larger churches, such as the Minster or the various monasteries.

As well as the local provision there were the monasteries and nunneries in and around York. The largest monastery was St Mary's Abbey, which had recovered from the defection of some of the monks to found Fountains Abbey, and it was to become the largest Benedictine monastery in the north of England. There were also smaller monasteries in York. St Andrew's priory on Fishergate belonged to the

Gilbertine order, which was the only medieval monastic order to be founded by an Englishman, St Gilbert. A small nunnery, St Clements, was located just outside the walls beside the River Ouse. There were also some hospitals, notably St Leonard's hospital and, for lepers, St Nicholas's hospital. As well as the monasteries and institutions themselves, other monasteries in the region owned houses and property in York, such as the great Yorkshire Cistercian monasteries of Rievaulx, Fountains, and Bylands.

This established pattern was to change dramatically upon the arrival of the friars. The friars also lived in communities based upon rules of living, but instead of favouring the isolation of the Cistercian monks, the friars deliberately settled in towns so they could preach and minister to the local population – rich and poor alike. There were four main orders of friars, the first of which to arrive in England were the Franciscans and the Dominicans. The Franciscan Order was based on the teachings of St Francis, and the Dominican Order was based on the teachings of St Dominic. The Dominicans arrived in York in 1227 and King Henry III gave them land in Toft Green within the city walls, as well as timber from the Forest of Galtres with which to construct their buildings. The Franciscans followed soon after, arriving *c.* 1230. By the middle of the century the other two orders of friars, the Augustinians and the Carmelites, had also settled in York. York was also a regional centre for each of the orders and for the Dominicans the city was the venue for the national meeting for the order, called a Provincial Chapter, for the years 1235, 1246, 1256, 1275, 1280, 1306 and 1329. The numbers of monks and friars in York is very hard to judge, though a best guess for the number of friars in York between the 1290s and 1330s – the heyday of York's prosperity – were fifty Dominician, forty-five Fransciscan, thirty Carmelite and thirty-five Augustinian friars. Although few in number, their distinctive habits, each order having a different colour, meant that they were a common sight in the city.

ARCHITECTURE

The period between 1066 and 1290 witnessed three great architectural styles: the Norman introduction of the Romanesque style, then, *c.* 1180 came the development of the Early English style and finally, *c.* 1240, the creation of the Gothic style. Examples of all these styles can be most clearly seen in the churches of the region. The supreme example of the Romanesque style in the north of England is Durham Cathedral, whilst within York the typical round headed and carved Romanesque doorways can be seen on the churches of St Margaret's Walmgate, St Denys's Walmgate and as part of the tower of St Nicholas's church in Lawrence Street. In the Yorkshire Museum there is the reconstructed Romanesque doorway of St Mary's Abbey. The Minster was also at one time a fabulous Romanesque church, fragments of which can still be seen in the crypt and with decoration similar to that in Durham Cathedral. The sole piece of domestic architecture that can be seen from this date is in a small yard off Stonegate. The 'Norman House' was discovered in 1939 during the destruction of a later building.

The second style was the Early English style which was made possible by the use of pointed arches, rather than the round arches of the Romanesque. Pointed arches allowed windows to be taller and thinner. Within the Minster the magnificent towering 'Five Sisters' window of the north transept is an excellent example. Just outside York, in Skelton, is the almost perfect survival of an Early English church. The final style is that of the Gothic style which developed from the Early English – the windows became larger and the stone tracery within the windows became ever more elaborate. The huge west window of York Minster has Gothic tracery designed as a heart, which is known as the 'Heart of York'.

York's Defences c. 1250

By the middle of the thirteenth century York had formidable defences, with two castles, a circuit of walls almost around the city with the king's Fishpool forming an impassable quagmire which completed the circuit. Initially York Castle was made out of wood, but in 1228 the castle was severely damaged (probably by high winds) and following a visit by King Henry III in 1244 the castle was rebuilt in stone. The work consisted of building in stone the walls, towers, gates, bridges, two halls, a chapel, a kitchen and a prison and the total cost came to £2450.

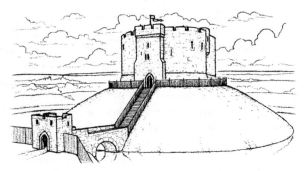

Clifford's Tower as it may have been in the fourteenth century

Today the visible part of this rebuilding is Clifford's Tower, which is the structure on top of the motte or mound. It has four 'lobes' and is an unusual design, with only three other similar designs known, two in France and the other at Pontefract, south of York.

The reason for the structure being called Clifford's Tower has puzzled historians through the ages. During the Middle Ages it was known as the 'Great Tower' and the first recorded use of the name of Clifford's Tower was in 1596. One reason that it may have been connected to the Clifford family was that in 1322 Roger de Clifford was hanged by chains from the wall of the tower for opposing Edward II, however, it was probably because the Clifford family claimed that they were the hereditary constables of the tower.

Even though York was not involved in any direct attack, its strategic and regional importance meant that it had strong defences. As well as the military function of the castle, the castle was a focus of law and order, and was also a base for the sheriff of Yorkshire. The county courts were based within the bailey, with the associated prison. Criminals and traitors were often hanged from the battlements of Clifford's Tower as a visible deterrent.

The defensive walls and ditches around the city were of variable quality. Some walls had survived from the Roman times in various states of disrepair, though the walls behind the Minster, which had been part of the Roman Legionary fortress were probably in better condition than most. There is little detail about the walls, though there is a reference to the 'walls' or defences at the bottom of Walmgate being no more than a hedge. The gates and bars however were crucial both in terms of defence and trade. It can be argued that the walls of the city were as much about funnelling trade through the bars as about defence, for it was at the bars that tolls were collected for bringing goods into the city. Originally all the bars probably had a barbican on the front, though now only the barbican on Walmgate Bar remains. This feature allowed goods to enter at one end, with a closed gate ahead. The rear gate was then closed and the goods and people were confined until payment was made. The inner door could then open and the people could enter the city.

The changes that the Normans made from 1066 onwards and then the steady growth of the prosperity and independence of its citizens and churches formed a strong foundation for York's future wealth during the following centuries. However, ultimately its strategic location near the Scottish border was to be the deciding factor in making York the true capital of England for a short time in the following century.

CHAPTER FOUR

The Golden Age of York, 1272–1485

Edward I (1272–1307): The Hammer of the Scots

In 1272 King Henry III died and his eldest son Edward was crowned. Three decisions by King Edward I would have a direct impact upon York: the expulsion of the Jewish community, the creation of Kingston upon Hull as a trading port down river and the arrival of the king and court, which effectively made York the capital of England.

THE EXPULSION OF THE JEWS 1290

In 1190 the Jewish community of York had been massacred, but the community revived and continued living in the city. However, as the thirteenth century progressed the English kings increasingly saw the Jewish communities throughout England as a source of revenue and imposed ever more crippling taxes upon them. The scale of this taxation can be seen by the accounts of one of the most important Jews in England, Aaron of York. At the height of his financial power he had leant money across fourteen counties in England and not only had a magnificent house in York, but also one in London as well. From 1243 the king, Henry III, taxed the Jews ever more heavily. Aaron alone paid approximately £20,000 to the king in seven years. During the 1250s he was financially ruined and died in obscurity in 1268. Aaron's story was an extreme case of what was happening across England. Jews who were unable to pay the exorbitant sums were imprisoned. By 1290, when Edward I ordered all the Jews to be expelled from England, the communities in York and elsewhere in England were penniless shadows of their former selves. What happened to the individuals when they left York, and then England, is unknown.

However, the amount of information about the Jewish community dramatically increased between 1982 and 1983 when archaeologists discovered the Jewish cemetery in an area just outside the city walls called Jewbury. The archaeologists excavated 475 burials which were neatly laid out and, unlike a Christian cemetery, no grave was dug into another. Whilst there were a few individuals with wounds caused by weapons, there was no sign of the massacre of 1190. A license was first granted to the Jews of York for their own cemetery in York in 1177; prior to this Jews from York were buried in London. In 1177 the cemetery was opened and it was not only the community of York who buried their dead there, but also those of Lincoln, Northampton and Stamford in Lincolnshire, although gradually these other Jewish communities gained cemeteries of their own. The look of the cemetery was that of a pleasant garden, and there would have been tombstones indicating who was buried where. Following the expulsion of the Jews in 1290 the land was seized and sold for £15 and gradually the cemetery was forgotten until it once again gained prominence through archaeological excavations.

TIME, TIDES AND KINGSTON UPON HULL

The second decision instigated by Edward I had a much longer term impact upon the city of York and its fortunes – the creation of Kingston upon Hull by a royal charter in 1299. Within a few decades Hull had become a major shipping centre and port.

Before this York had been the primary port of the river systems stretching across Yorkshire. The city was ranked seventh in importance of the English ports of the east and south coasts in 1203–4 and in the 1290s, sixty-nine shipwrights were living in York, more than London, which had fifty, Southampton and Portsmouth which both had thirty-eight and Ipswich which had thirty-five. Yet York as a port had some major problems. The most intractable was the tides. The River Ouse which flows through York today always looks full and deep but this is because of Naburn Lock downstream which was built in 1757. Before the building of the lock York was at the mercy of the tides from the North Sea coming up the River Ouse. At certain times of the year if a ship missed sailing with the tide it could be stranded in York for up to two weeks.

The tidal variance was much less of an issue at Kingston upon Hull as it was on the Humber estuary and as the trading advantages of the tide and the dock facilities became apparent, more and more ships sailed from the new town, at the expense of York. However, even though York's status as a port began to diminish, political events meant that it was to become briefly the capital of England.

York: England's Capital

The turning point in York's fortune, which raised it to be briefly the capital of England, was the death of the Scottish King Alexander III in 1286. For most of the century before 1286 relations between England and Scotland had been relatively peaceful, but Alexander III's death left a power vacuum in Scotland. Two main rivals vied for the throne – John Bailliol and Robert the Bruce. Both were powerful magnates with extensive estates in Scotland and the north of England. (It was John Bailliol's father, also called John, who was rich enough to found Bailliol College in Oxford University). Edward supported Bailliol but his efforts to impose a settlement failed and through the actions of William Wallace and then Robert the Bruce, the Scottish nobility refused to bow to Edward's will.

From 1296 onwards Edward sought to impose his will by force. To do this he not only collected together an impressively large army, but he also moved the Exchequer and Chancery, the two departments at the heart of government, northwards from London to York. They arrived in York in 1298 and returned back to London in 1304.

Even though the king himself was only sporadically in York, the city had become the nation's capital. Soldiers, administrators and courtiers all came to York either heading north to Scotland or on government business. The massive influx of people – both rich and poor – and the resultant trade must have improved the economic fortunes of many merchants in the city. Some of the people of York also had a direct hand in the fighting as forty crossbowmen from the city were sent to defend Stirling castle in 1304.

The fighting in Scotland was not the swift and decisive victory that Edward had hoped for and in 1307 the elderly Edward I died as he was making his way for another offensive against the Scots. It was his wish that his son, Edward II, should continue in the fight to subdue the Scots.

Edward II (1307–27) proved to be in a very different mould to his father and was far from being the wily political leader and great military commander his father was. Edward II disliked warfare and preferred the easy pleasures of the court. In the early years of his reign Edward half-heartedly attempted to impose his will upon the Scots and so was frequently in the north and in York. However, his schemes for domination over Scotland were crushed by Robert the Bruce's shattering victory over the English army at Bannockburn on 24 June 1314.

The resulting power of Scotland after Bannockburn meant that Yorkshire and the whole of the north of England was under threat from rapid raids or full blown invasion. In 1319 the Scots rode into York-shire. A rapidly assembled force, including the mayor of York, Nicholas Fleming, rode out to meet them. The Scots devastated the inexperienced English army and drove them back into a river. Nicholas Fleming has the dubious distinction of being the only mayor of York to be killed in action. Another Scottish raid in 1322 reached the outskirts of the city and caused havoc in the Bootham area, but the citizens shut the gates and the Scots retreated. In the following year a truce was agreed between Robert the Bruce and Edward II, a truce negotiated in the archbishop of York's palace down the river at Bishopthorpe.

SHOOTING SCOTSMEN

There is a popular notion in York that there is a medieval city by-law which allows for the shooting of Scotsmen by bow and arrow on St George's Field. However, this is York's very own local myth for there is no evidence of any such statute ever been passed. Although it is known widely throughout the city, it is wrong. The closest statute refers to the barring of Scotsmen from the council chamber at a particularly sensitive time between England and Scotland.

The Abolition of The Knights Templar 1312

The Knights Templar (properly called the Military Order of the Knights of the Temple of Solomon) were one of the military religious orders which had grown and flourished during the Crusades to protect pilgrims and to fight actively for the Christian cause. In order to fund their activities a vast European network of properties had been developed which included farms, houses and mills. The Templars owned a great deal of property in Yorkshire, and in York the Order owned a range of properties, the most important of which was St George's chapel and two water mills at the base of the dam blocking the River Foss by the castle.

Despite their power and wealth the Templars came under suspicion right across Europe for heresy and rumours abounded about what the secretive Order really believed. Witnesses were called and gave evidence that in reality the Templars not only denied Christ, but insulted him and carried out sacrilegious acts. All the Templars in England were sent to one of three locations: London, Lincoln or York: twenty-four Templars ended up in York Castle. Following their confession each of the twenty-four agreed to abandon the Order and were placed in monasteries. Others in Europe were not so lucky and many were tortured and some burned at the stake.

Their property in Yorkshire and York was seized and either kept in the king's hands or sold. It is not known what became of the mills, but St George's Chapel in York remained and became a royal chapel in 1311. During the sixteenth century the chapel was given to York corporation, but was eventually pulled down in 1856.

Riot, Marriage and the Scots

In 1327 King Edward II was deposed (reputedly by a having a red hot poker thrust into his bowels so no visible mark remained) and in his place his son, Edward III (1327–77), was made king. Even though he was only fifteen years of age he was a dynamic king and immediately set about establishing York as the city from which to launch an invasion of Scotland.

In May 1327 Edward III arrived in York to supervise the next stage of the Scottish wars and repulse a Scottish invasion. The king stayed in the friary of the Franciscans which was situated between the castle and the River Ouse. Also in the friary was the queen mother and her court of sixty ladies. On Trinity Sunday the king held court at the friary, a great and colourful occasion attended by five hundred knights, followed by a banquet.

Included in the celebrations were a group of nobles and their soldiers from Hainault who were involved with the Scottish wars because Edward III was betrothed to Philippa of Hainault. During the celebrations a running battle occurred between a large group of archers from Lincolnshire who were fighting soldiers from Hainault. The fight went back and forth and as many as eighty soldiers were killed. The turbulent situation resulted in the king sending the contingent from Hainault home.

The military situation resolved itself by the Scots retreating in advance of Edward's army, so Edward returned to York. The following year, on 24 January 1328, the king and Philippa of Hainault were married in York Minster. The marriage was attended by virtually every leading member of the English aristocracy. Edward and Philippa's connection with the Minster survives, because their son, William of Hatfield, who died as a child, was buried in the Minster. His tomb can still be seen today in the north choir aisle. Edward, like his grandfather and father before him, moved the government to York. With the king in the city, the chancery located at St Mary's Abbey and the exchequer, in York castle, York was once again the capital of England.

In the early years of campaigning against the Scots Edward III was successful, but never decisively so and his attention began to turn to a much greater prize, that of the French crown. As military expeditions against the Scots faltered in the 1330s so Edward's military ambitions turned to attacking the French. The initial campaign against France in 1337 started the Hundred Years War, which finally ended in 1453. For almost forty years of fighting against the Scots York had been the hub of government and court life, but after 1338 this ended with the government departments once more moving south to London. Parliament had gathered fifteen times in York between 1298 and 1335: after 1335 it was never again in York

The Black Death 1349–50

During 1347 and 1348 a plague had been moving north-westwards through Europe, devastating communities as it went. Plague was a common feature of life in the Middle Ages and there had been numerous plagues in the previous centuries but none was so devastating or virulent as the Black Death. The plague probably first arrived at the small Dorset port of Melcombe when a ship from Gascony arrived and unloaded its wares, which included an accidental and wholly unwelcome consignment of ship's rats and their associated fleas. The men of Melcombe became infected and the plague rapidly spread. Nothing could stop the advance of the plague and it had reached Yorkshire in March 1349 and Scotland by 1350. Estimates vary but the plague proably killed between a third and a half of the total population of England.

The horror of the plague was well recorded by contemporaries and a monk at Rochester in Kent wrote:

> nobody could be found who would bear the corpses to the grave. Men and women carried their own children on their shoulders to the church and threw them into the common pit. From these pits such an appalling stench was given off that scarcely anyone dared even to walk beside the cemeteries.

In Hertfordshire some graffiti is scratched into the church tower: 'Wretched, terrible, violent. Only the remnants of the people are left to tell the tale'

The devastation caused by the Black Death in York is only revealed in administrative documents. Almost half the parish priests of the city died and the number of craftsmen and traders made freemen of York – normally about fifty a year – increased to 212 in 1350-51 as new freemen were created to fill the gaps of those who died. The Black Death was not the last plague and there were others in York throughout the centuries and references to plague causing high mortality rates occur in 1391, 1429, 1436, 1438, 1459, 1467, 1471-2, 1474, 1483, 1505-6 and 1508-9. Whilst these were devastating in their right, none compared to the severity of the Black Death.

'Great Animosities': St Mary's Abbey and the Citizens of York, 1354

In 1354 King Edward III negotiated a final truce between the monks of St Mary's Abbey and the mayor and citizens of York. The dispute originated in a disagreement about which side owned the jurisdiction of Bootham. The matter came to a head in 1264 when the citizens murdered a number of St Mary's community and burned several houses in Bootham. To restore peace the abbot paid £100 to the citizens. A peace was agreed in 1275, but it was too one-sided in favour of St Mary's and the discord continued. It was after the agreement that the abbot decided that the abbey needed considerable protection and had a high stone defensive wall built around the site. It is this wall that can still be seen today along Marygate. Further defences in the form of ditches and strengthening of the wall occurred in 1315–6. The citizens saw this as an insult and attempted to fill in the ditches and destroy the wall, whereupon it collapsed, killing five of them. The dispute over who owned Bootham continued. In 1343 the citizens attacked monks and in 1350 the citizens blocked food supplies to the abbey which came up the River Ouse and threatened to crucify the monks. The situation was getting seriously out of hand and once again the king stepped in and negotiated a new agreement in 1354 which restored Bootham to the citizens whilst keeping some land in the abbey's possession. This arrangement took the heat out of the situation and there were no more incidents.

THE CHURCHES

During the Middle Ages the power and wealth of the church became immense and in York the church was spiritually all powerful. However there were small groups of people who followed other beliefs in Europe and the main group in England was that of the Lollards who took their precepts mainly from the Bible rather than the Catholic clergy. However, the Lollards were few in number, persecuted and mainly based in the south and the Midlands and had little influence in the north. This is ironic, given that the main person behind the heresy was John Wycliffe, who originated from the small Yorkshire village of Wycliffe. He later became a Dominican friar in York and it was there that he received holy orders in 1350–1.

In York the largest and most important church was the Minster. The day to day running of the Minster and its properties was undertaken by the dean and chapter. The chapter consisted of thirty-six canons who all possessed churches and properties – called prebends – around Yorkshire. The wealthiest prebend was that of Masham which was worth £120 a year. As well as the dean and chapter who controlled the administration of the Minster and its estates, there was the archbishop who oversaw both the diocese of York and the archdiocese of York, which included the dioceses of York, Durham and Carlisle. The archbishops were often previously important men in government and were rewarded with the post of archbishop – between 1374–1500 five of the archbishops were appointed when they were also chancellor of England. Their government post meant that they often journeyed with the king or were away from York for long periods on other business.

As well as the Minster, with its property and lands across the city, there were numerous other churches scattered around York. These included the Benedictine monasteries of St Mary's Abbey, Holy Trinity Priory in Micklegate, the churches and lands of the Gilbertine canons in Fishergate and the St Clement's nunnery in Clementhorpe. The wealthier monasteries owned substantial land and properties in and around York. St Mary's Abbey owned houses and land, all of which was outside the jurisdiction of the city. As well as York based churches, the wealth and trading links of the city resulted in other monasteries holding land and property in York. The prior of Nostell Priory owned a property in Stonegate, which has been restored and renovated and is now Barley Hall. The abbeys of Fountains, Jervaulx and Byland all had wool storage houses in Clifton, a northern suburb of York.

The Poll Taxes and the Peasant's Revolt

Between 1377 and 1381 three national poll taxes were levied by the Government, but only the 1377 poll tax returns have survived in quantity. The records form an invaluable source for historians to gauge the size of the national and local populations and the 1377 records for York list 7,248 lay tax payers. The poll tax of 1377 required a set payment of four pence per person over the age of fourteen, without regard of their income, except that 'real beggars' were excluded. Once other groups have been added in, for example children under fourteen, 'real beggars' and the clergy, the total population has been estimated at between 11,000 and 15,000 people. Only London was bigger in size and population, estimated at *c.* 50,000 people.

However, it was the last poll tax in 1381 which sparked the peasant's revolt – the greatest uprising of the Middle Ages. The rebels of Kent and East Anglia led by Wat Tyler and John Ball marched to London. They proved to be a serious threat to the stability of the kingdom and it was only the boy king Richard II's bravery in riding out and speaking with the rebels that caused them to disperse. There were swift reprisals of the ringleaders. The main rebel force was in the south but an ex-mayor of York, recently ousted from power decided to regain his position and marched on the city with some of his supporters. The move failed and he was never mayor again.

Richard II (1377–99) and York

Richard II visited York six times in total, the first time in 1387. During this visit he gave a sword to the city, with the honour that it could be carried, point upright in procession, unless the king himself was present, otherwise the point was to be carried downwards.

Further visits in 1393 and 1396 led to greater and greater concessions by the king. In May 1396 Richard granted York's most significant charter, which promoted the city, and the area to the west of the city called the Ainsty, to the status of a county in its own right: 'the county of the city of York'. By 1397 the sheriff of Yorkshire's jurisdiction over the city had been replaced by two annually elected sheriffs, controlled by the mayor. These changes signified York's importance as a major trading and mercantile city at the height of its prosperity.

The connection between Richard II and York grew strong in the minds of York citizens and there grew a legend (since dispelled) that Richard had special regard for the city above all other cities in the kingdom. The legend grew because of Richard's frequent visits to York, the charter of 1396, that he buried his son in the Minster, and that he created the title the duke of York. The first person to be granted the title was his uncle in 1385, who also received lands from the crown to the yearly value of £1000.

THE 'MARTYRDOM' OF ARCHBISHOP OF SCROPE IN 1405

Richard II's downfall in 1399 was the result of his overthrow by the powerful nobleman Henry Bolingbroke. Henry became King Henry IV (1399-1413), the first of the kings of the House of Lancaster. Richard II had been a great favourite of the York authorities and the anger of York citizens lay simmering whilst Henry IV secured the country. A series of rebellions were launched against Henry, the most significant of which was the Glendower Rebellion of 1403. Glendower declared himself king of Wales and gained the backing of the earl of Northumberland, Henry Percy. The rebellion was crushed but Northumberland was spared. However in 1405 rebellion flared up once more, again being led by the earl of Northumberland and his son Henry 'Harry Hotspur' Percy. This time the rebellion directly involved York.

Richard Scrope, archbishop of York, actively joined the rebellion and went about the city proclaiming the rebel cause. He also preached in the Minster about the poverty of York's citizens and the burden of royal taxation. His influence led 'almost all the citizens of York capable of bearing arms' to join the rebels. King Henry IV did not stand idly by and with decisive action tricked or harried the leaders, who were gradually defeated. The king himself arrived at the archbishop's palace at Bishopthorpe just outside York, arrested Archbishop Scrope and summarily executed him in a nearby field. Even though Scrope had been involved in traitorous events, the killing of an archbishop by the king was not forgotten by the citizens and his tomb in the Minster became a shrine for local people. Later in life Henry IV became paralysed by illness and it was said that this was God's punishment for the killing of the archbishop.

The People

Compared to the quieter, less populous countryside York was a bustling teeming metropolis. There was a wide range of trades in the city which catered for the everyday needs of its citizens. An insight into the most prominent of trades is given by the Freeman's Register. It was started in 1272 and is the first record of the men, and occasionally women, who were merchants and had gained the freedom of the city.

A person had to have the status of a freeman to be able to buy and sell goods in the city and there were three ways of becoming a freeman: inheritance, purchase or apprenticeship. The richest men of the city were the merchants who traded in goods across Europe. Trade across the North Sea was particularly lucrative and a key port in the Baltic was Danzig, a particular favourite with York merchants. When a count is made of the freemen in the Register the greatest number of traders were those dealing with wool or cloth, with a large number of master weavers and tailors. Following this group were the group of metal-workers, a diverse group who included goldsmiths, silversmiths and blacksmiths, as well as makers of armour and spurs. The street name of Spurriergate is named after the spur makers in York. The evidence for the importance of the bell makers of York can still be seen in the Minster where there is the bellfounders' window.

Those who did not have the freedom, or came from beyond the city boundaries, were termed 'aliens' or foreigners. As York was a market place for many nations and a significant port, aliens from oversees were a small but noticeable group. The largest contingent were known as 'Deutsch', a term which included people from Holland to Austria, whilst others came from Gascony and even Iceland. Overseas traders sometimes settled in York, and one such was the German goldsmith John Colan. It was a Dutchman, Fridericus Freez, who first brought the printing press to York, so starting a long tradition of printing in the city.

As well as the richer merchants of the city, other citizens are known, through the excellent and detailed medieval records which survive for York. There are many incidental references to legal cases, punishments and details of life in the city such as the time when one of the serjeants of the city, John Nicolson went to arrest a glover, Richard Davias. Richard grabbed the prison keys and hit Nicolson over the head with them. Another incident which happened in 1486 concerned a gathering of members of the Minster clergy and others 'to the number of 30 persons' who assembled riotously and 'by night hurt certain persons'. At the same time a separate group dressed 'in the manner of war ... shot many arrows against the Sheriffs ... coming to them for the conservation of the peace'. Unfortunately the outcome to the case and what happened to the rioters has not survived.

As well as the general population of York there was also a constant stream of visitors. Many came on church business, either to attend the church courts or to visit St William's shrine. Most pilgrims came and went without any mention within the records, but one pilgrim later had her life written down. Margery Kempe came to York with her husband in 1413 during the height of summer and arrived 'with a bottle of beer in her hand' whilst her husband carried a cake. During a second visit she entered the Minster and caused a commotion by her loud weeping and crying, so much so that she was sent to the archbishop to be questioned about her beliefs.

THE GUILDS

There were two sorts of guilds in York, trade guilds which regulated the activities of a particular craft or trade, and religious guilds which were for the spiritual benefit of their members both alive and – through prayers – dead. The number of trade guilds varied through the centuries but by the fifteenth century one list records eighty and it is from this century that large number of the ordinances, or rules, of the crafts have survived. In 1495 the Ordinances of the Porters dictate that there were to be only sixteen porters who could carry items between the river and various stated streets for a penny. Turfs are specifically mentioned – a hundred small turfs or sixty great turfs make a 'burden' for which can be charged a penny. The Ordinances of the Drapers in 1492 were largely concerned with stopping 'foreign' drapers (ie drapers who were not Freemen of the City) trading illegally in the city. One such group specifically mentioned were the men of the Lake District town of Kendal who sold their goods from their rooms in inns and lodgings rather than the Thursday market.

Despite the numerous rules laid down, the number of guilds meant that there was potential for joint co-operation or dispute. The trades who used animals skins in their work – tanners, glovers, parchment makers, girdlers, curriers and cordwainers – all grouped together to check the quality of the skins coming into the city. The overlap between the trades meant that disputes could arise and in 1490 there was a major dispute between the tilers and the masons over a building project. The tilers had foreseen trouble as they were undertaking a task normally reserved for the masons and so had asked the corporation for protection. If it was given it wasn't effective because it was alleged that a tiler, John Patrik, was murdered by two masons, the master mason of York Minster William Hyndley and Christopher Horner. Despite this, the tilers continued and their finished work can still be seen today as the brick and tile building called the Red Tower on Foss Islands Road.

The guilds were authorised by the city authorities – who were often guild members themselves – to be responsible for the quality of goods and workmanship. The mayor and council were the ultimate arbiters in any disputes within or between guilds, and if necessary could dissolve a guild. Each guild had a hierarchy and had 'searchers', who had the power to make inspections of everything from the raw materials to the finished goods. There was an insistence by all the guilds upon good workmanship. The guilds also had control of apprentices who often had to serve a seven year apprenticeship

The most important guilds were very rich and powerful and to this day evidence for a few survives in the city in the form of their guildhalls. The two best known are the guildhalls of the Merchant Adventurer's, whose formal entrance is in Fossgate, though a spectacular view can be seen from Piccadilly, and the Taylor's, whose hall is in St Andrewgate.

The religious guilds were founded with the aim of caring for the burial and remembrance of their deceased members. This could be achieved by an elaborate burial ceremony immediately after death, with a procession, mourners and bells, and then a continual round of prayers for the dead and anniversary services. The most important religious guild of all, the Corpus Christi Guild was founded in 1408 to celebrate the Feast of Corpus Christi. The Corpus Christi Guild was one of the most powerful in York and between its foundation and closure in 1546 the guild had nearly 17,000 members drawn both from the upper echelons of York society and further afield, including archbishops of York and powerful regional nobility, such as the Cliffords, Latimers and Scropes.

THE MYSTERY PLAYS

The guilds were also responsible for one of the glories of medieval York culture, the Mystery Plays. The name 'mystery' comes from the

Merchant Adventurers' Hall

'mysteries' of each of the guilds professions, but this name was only introduced in the sixteenth century. Previously they were probably known as the Corpus Christi plays and were performed on one the great medieval Christian festivals, the Feast of Corpus Christi. (The date of Corpus Christi is sixty days after Easter.)

The plays were usually performed by guilds aptly chosen for each element: the shipwrights' pageant was 'the building of Noah's Ark', the vintners performed the marriage of Cana at which Christ turned water into wine, and the Guild of Builders performed the creation story. Some of the associations are macabre, the pinners performed the crucifixion where Christ is nailed to the cross and the guild of butchers performed the death of Christ. Of course the primary purpose was to glorify God and tell the Biblical story from creation to the Last Judgement, but human nature meant that each of the guilds vied with each other to produce the best play and gain prestige. However, sometimes animosity spilt over and the cordwainers (producers of the agony and betrayal of Christ) rioted against the carpenters in 1419, and then twice with the weavers in 1490 and 1492. Whilst the plays were a source of prestige and demonstration of power, they were also burdensome upon the guilds for not only did they have to stage them, they also had to pay 'pageant-silver' to maintain them.

The earliest detailed records of the plays was written down by a civic official called Roger Burton who wrote down a list of the mystery plays in 1415. In his list there are fifty-one plays. However the text of the plays, written down *c.*1430–40 only gives forty-eight plays, each produced by a separate guild. This text however incorporates elements which are much older, stretching back into the fourteenth century and it is known that the plays were being performed as a group in 1376. There are even earlier references to plays being performed in York and there is an early reference to plays in York in 1220–5 when there is the note in the Statute Book of York Minster:

> Item, one will contrive stars with all things pertaining to them except the rushes . . . : one on Christmas night for the shepherds and two on Epiphany night if the presentation of the three kings be done.

The Mystery Plays were very popular with citizens and visitors alike and in 1398 King Richard II watched them. Each of the forty-eight plays were performed on wagons which were rolled through the streets to separate stations. The route that they followed is well known: down Micklegate, across Ouse Bridge, down Coney Street, down Stonegate and ending in St Helen's Square. At each of the stations where the wagons stopped there was specially constructed seating on scaffolding for those rich enough to hire seats.

Architecture and Stained Glass

The wealth of the city in the thirteenth and fourteenth centuries created magnificent architecture and has left a stunning legacy of medieval stained glass.

The single greatest building in York, which also contains one of the greatest collections of medieval stained glass in the country, is York Minster. Over the centuries the Minster has been added to and changed. The first Norman Romanesque building was demolished section by section as new building campaigns were implemented. Archbishop Roger of Pont l'Évêque rebuilt the choir, which was then rebuilt again in the fourteenth century. The magnificent Chapter House was probably started in the 1260s or 1270s. The building of the Minster was not without incident and in 1407 part of the central tower collapsed, probably as a result of changes being made to the vaulting of the choir. The master mason, William Colchester, arrived from Westminster Abbey and designed a new central tower, which stands to this day. The visible two west towers and the central tower were therefore comparatively late additions being finished after 1450. The last major building campaign in the Minster's history finished in 1472.

The earliest remains of a house in York are of Norman design and lie in a yard off Stonegate. However, this building is only fragmentary and the earliest domestic buildings which are still used date from 1316. Formerly known as 'Lady Row' they were built so that their rents could fund priests within Holy Trinity Goodramgate. Medieval houses from the following decades and centuries are common in York. Many are masked by the fact that they have newer, Georgian, frontages put on in the eighteenth century, but behind the façade lie the timber beams of medieval buildings.

As well as the houses and shops there are other medieval buildings, including the guild halls, the most impressive of which is the Merchant's Adventurer's Hall. It has been described as the finest medieval guildhall in Europe. The hall was built between 1357 and 1368 originally as a hospital, but later became the meeting place of the Guild of Merchant Adventurers. Until recently it was thought that the building was built on previously unused land – it therefore came as a considerable surprise to discover through archaeological investigation that under the present structure were the foundations of an older building. What the first building was has yet to be determined.

The medieval stained glass of York is a truly outstanding collection and rivals any other town in Europe. One of the most common reasons for paying for stained glass was the self-aggrandisement of York's most prominent citizens. Donor windows, where the donor and family can be seen kneeling at the bottom, are common. Some trades and guilds also paid for windows. In the Minster there is a window in the nave which had large numbers of bells depicted, aptly given by the Bell Founders. The greatest single window is that at the east end of the

Angels and Devils in medieval stained glass

Minster which depicts two Biblical narrative stories, the first is the creation, and the second is the story in Revelation. Its sheer size means that the details are lost and the only way to see the window properly is to take binoculars! The window was paid for by Bishop Skirlaw of Durham who had been elected by the dean and chapter, but their choice was over-ridden by King Richard II who placed Richard Scrope as archbishop. After Scrope's execution by King Henry IV, Skirlaw tried to gain the office of archbishop again. In 1405 Skirlaw paid John Thornton of Coventry to glaze the east window, a feat which Thornton finished in three years. Skirlaw died before obtaining the post of archbishop, but his gift has meant his name has been remembered as one of the great patrons of the Minster. Skirlaw himself is depicted in the window – in the centre amongst portrayals of legendary and historical figures from York's past.

The skill and humour of the stained glass artists can also be seen in much of the glass throughout York. At the bottom of a window in the nave of the Minster is a depiction of a monkey's funeral with other animals in attendance. Smaller still is a charming depiction in the Zouche chapel on a single piece of glass of a wren watching a spider in its web. From the spider to the vast east window the glass, even today, fires the wonder and admiration of the visitor.

Wars of the Roses

For over a hundred years the kings of England had been fighting for the throne of France. The culmination came when Henry VI (1422–61), was crowned king of France as a baby. Unfortunately for the English cause Henry's adherents could not keep power and after being defeated by the military genius of Joan of Arc, the English party lost power. In later life Henry VI became mad, an event which sparked the Wars of the Roses. Into the vacuum stepped Richard, duke of York who effectively governed the country whilst Henry was ill. However Henry regained his sanity and with his queen, Margaret of Anjou, fought Richard for the throne. Both Henry and Richard claimed descent from Edward III – Henry was descended from Edward III's sixth child John of Gaunt, duke of Lancaster, whilst Richard was descended from Edward III's seventh child, Edmund of Langley, duke of York. As each county had a different coloured rose (white for Yorkshire and red for Lancashire) the ensuing battles became known as the Wars of the Roses. However, whilst the title is an evocative one, both sides had lands spread throughout England and initially the Lancastrian cause was strong in Yorkshire, though this was later to change.

HEADS AND PAPER CROWNS

During the wars the city of York itself did not militarily play a prominent part, though it was used as a symbol of power by both sides. Richard's Yorkist party suffered a devastating blow at the battle of Wakefield in December 1460 when he was killed. To show their dominance the Lancastrians cut the heads off Richard and his sons, put paper crowns on them and stuck them on Micklegate Bar, which was the most important gateway in the city as it lead to London. Richard's other sons, Edward and Richard, fought on to wrest the throne from Henry VI. Edward soon had his revenge at the battle of Towton.

THE BATTLE OF TOWTON 1461

On Palm Sunday 1461 Britain's 'bloodiest battle' was fought a few miles from York at Towton between the Yorkist king, King Edward, and the Lancastrian army of King Henry VI. Edward had been crowned a few weeks earlier and with two crowned kings of England opposing each other the stakes could not have been higher. Edward's powerbase was in London and to fight his Lancastrian opponents he marched north into Yorkshire.

Once King Edward's forces arrived in Yorkshire there were a series of skirmishes and minor battles, but finally the two huge armies met at Towton. At the time it was estimated that 28,000 soldiers took part and Shakespeare, writing over hundred years later, described it as like a contest between the wind and tide of a mighty sea, so large were the opposing armies. Even though the Lancastrians had a slight advantage in their position, the wind was to become a deciding factor. During the battle a snowstorm raged, blowing from the Yorkist lines into the faces of the Lancastrians. The Yorkist archers took advantage of this and their arrows were carried into the Lancastrian lines whilst the Lancastrian arrows fell short. With the Lancastrian troops being massacred in their positions, they had no choice but to attack. The sheer weight of Lancastrian troops forced the Yorkists onto the defensive and there ensued a massive hand-to-hand conflict. Gradually the Lancastrians got the upper hand and the Yorkists despaired and were on the point of collapse, when just in time Yorkist reinforcements arrived and the battle decisively turned in the Yorkists' favour. The Lancastrians fled, being massacred as they did so. It was a massive Yorkist victory and secured King Edward's hold on the throne. It was reported that the local rivers ran red with blood for days after. As well as being Britain's bloodiest battle, the conflict was unusual for the length of time of the battle, which lasted from the rising of the sun until the 'tenth hour of the night'.

There the accounts may have ended, but in 1996 a mass grave was uncovered by archaeologists which contained at least thirty-eight men, whose average age was thirty. Many had obvious signs of weapon injuries, such as sword cuts to bones.

ARCHBISHOP NEVILLE'S FEAST, 1465

During the Wars of the Roses the single most powerful non-royal family in England was that of Richard Neville, the earl of Warwick. Warwick was so influential that whichever side he supported had enough power to become king, hence Warwick's nickname as 'Warwick the Kingmaker'. Warwick's brother was George Neville who was lord chancellor of England and bishop of Exeter, and in 1465 became archbishop of York. To impress the king with his power he held a most magnificent banquet at the archbishop's palace in Cawood. Approximately two thousand people were invited with the most important including dukes, bishops and earls, abbots and the dean and chapter of the Minster, the mayor of York, judges and barons and the king's ministers.

The feast was truly remarkable and included 104 oxen, 6 wild bulls, 1000 sheep, 2000 pigs, 500 stags, 4000 venison pasties (cold) and 1500 hot, 4000 pigeons, 2000 chickens and 2000 geese. The fish dishes consisted of 608 pikes and bream, 12 porpoises and seals, ling, haddock, eels, herrings, salmon, conger eel, trout, tench, barbel, minnows, shrimps, crabs and lobsters. Not surprisingly the feast gained a notoriety for its extravagance and elegance which has scarcely been matched since.

This remarkable display of wealth and extravagence did little to impress King Edward IV, who a few days later took away the position of chancellor from George Neville. A little while later Neville had his revenge when he captured the king, who in turn was released by Neville's brother, Warwick the Kingmaker. The tension between Edward IV and Warwick the Kingmaker grew to such an extent that Warwick left the country, only for him to return and proclaim Henry VI once again as king. The real power of the land lay in Warwick's hands so he reappointed his own brother, George, once again as chancellor of England.

The twists and turns of the war continued. At one point Edward was forced to flee abroad and when he returned to England he marched to York. The gates of Walmgate Bar were closed to him as he attempted to enter the city and were only opened when he acknowledged that

King Henry VI was the rightful king. However, Edward soon marched south and two battles in quick succession secured him as king. The first was the battle of Barnet during which Warwick the Kingmaker was killed. A month later Edward captured Henry VI and killed Henry's only son at the battle of Tewkesbury. Edward became undisputed king for the rest of his life and died peacefully in 1483. By the tradition Edward's eldest son, also called Edward, should have become king and if all had gone smoothly he would have been crowned as Edward V in 1483. Instead, however, his uncle and Edward's brother, Richard, duke of Gloucester, proclaimed himself as King Richard III.

DECLINE

By the late fifteenth century the city was in serious decline. A drop in trade had first been noticed by the weavers almost a century before from competition from weavers in the surrounding countryside. As the century progressed the decline became more pronounced, especially in the textile trades, such as dying, weaving and tailoring. One important task to produce cloth is that of fulling where the cloth is trampled into 'fuller's earth' to remove the oil, and in the late fifteenth century the fullers were also complaining of foreign competition. To try and reduce competition the city authorities banned cloth fulled by foreigners, and ordered that no wool was to be bought in or near the city unless cloth was to be made within the city.

The important leather industry of York had also reduced by the end of the century. The leather workers were split into a large range of separate trades including skinners, tanners, saddlers, cordwainers (makers of shoes). The leather production required the leather to be soaked in large vats of urine and the stench was such that the city authorities ordered that the leather workers practice their craft over the other side of the river. To this day one of the streets is called Tanner Row.

York as a port had also seen a reduction in trade. Edward I's creation of Kingston upon Hull had created a port which was not reliant on the tides as York was. By the fifteenth century York's status as an international port had markedly declined as merchants favoured Hull.

By the fifteenth century the council were complaining of the poverty of the city. The golden age of York's prosperity and national power and influence had passed. It was never to return.

Richard III (1483–1485)

Of all the kings of England Richard III stirs up the most heated debates. For centuries the standard view of Richard was that as portrayed in Shakespeare's *King Richard III* – that Richard was an evil hunchback who murdered and manipulated his way to the throne. However, during the twentieth century a powerful counter-movement claims that Richard was an able and misunderstood king.

The most heated arguments revolve around the fate of Edward IV's two sons, the Prince Edward and his younger brother Richard, duke of York. Their fate has never been determined but the last public sighting of the princes occurred during Richard's reign. Those who support King Richard claim there is no evidence to link him directly with the death of the princes, whilst his detractors point to the fact Richard seized the crown and proclaimed himself king. The debate swings backwards and forwards and it is probably fair to say that from this distance in time certainty one way or the other can never be proved.

Richard had close connections with York. He had married Anne Neville in 1481 and so inherited extensive northern estates which included Middleham Castle in the Dales and Sheriff Hutton, eight miles north-east of York. When Richard, duke of Gloucester, was crowned as king on 6 July 1483 the mayor and aldermen rode to Middleham Castle to make a presentation to Richard's only son, Edward, prince of Wales. They gave barrels of red and white wine, 6 cygnets, 6 heronshaws and 24 rabbits. Tragedy struck the following year with the death of Edward at Middleham Castle. Legend has it that his body was brought to Sheriff Hutton and buried in the parish church.

King Richard visited York several times and was widely supported and loved in the city. The longest visit by Richard, his queen and his son was for three weeks from 29 August 1483. He was met by the lord mayor and aldermen, dressed in scarlet, and at the entrance of the Minster King Richard was sprinkled with holy water. During their visit they progressed through York and the young prince was formally crowned as the Prince of Wales in the archbishop's palace which was then located behind the Minster. Richard's regard for York was such that he planned to be buried in the Minster. This was a radical reversal of tradition because the traditional burial place of English kings was at Westminster Abbey. Furthermore Richard had grand plans for the development of the Minster, aiming to add a further one hundred chaplains to pray for his soul in an enormous chantry chapel.

The citizens and corporation felt especially favoured by Richard and looked to him to offer some respite to the city's economic decline. Richard was described as the most 'special' of the 'good lords'. During the course of his reign the city actively supported Richard. In 1483 during Richard's visit to York he was given presents to the value of £450 but the city also aided his cause by sending soldiers in times of need. In October 1483 the city sent soldiers to help him and in the turbulent summer of 1485 when there were constant rumours of invasion the city mustered men for the king's defence. Then on 16 August news was heard of Henry Tudor's invasion and the city sent messengers to Richard at Nottingham to ask for instructions. A reply was received on the 19th that men should be sent and eighty were dispatched from York the same day. Before they could join Richard's forces he had been killed at the battle of Bosworth on 22 August. Although the body of York troops didn't fight, one man from York did, and returned to the city to report that: 'King Richard, late lawfully reigning over us, was through great treason ... piteously slain and murdered, to the great heaviness of the city'.

CHAPTER FIVE

Tudor and Stuart York, 1485–1689

During the Tudor and Stuart period York underwent great social and religious change. At the beginning of the period the city was still of national importance and was mourning the loss of a favoured king, Richard III. The city was full of churches which dominated the skyline, though the economic pressures resulted in a poorer city than in its heyday. In the following Tudor period the monasteries and friaries in York – and across England – were closed as a result of the Dissolution of the Monasteries. A second trauma was that of the Civil War when York was the strategic key to the north. By the end of the seventeenth century York had become a regionally important and socially elegant city but it was no longer of prime importance on the national stage.

Richard III's Memory and Henry VII

The death of Richard III on the battlefield of Bosworth in 1485 left the city corporation in some confusion. They had sent a contingent of soldiers to aid Richard, but they did not arrive in time to fight at the battle. The authorities of York were now left exposed for their loyalty and devotion to Richard III which meant that the new king, Henry VII (1485-1509), had to be placated. Henry visited in 1486 and to impress him and show the city's loyalty a magnificent series of events were organised. Outside Micklegate Bar children called 'joyfully "King Henry",' and then at Micklegate Bar there was a 'place in manner of a heaven, of great joy and angelical harmony'. The expertise of the guilds, well used to building scenery for the Mystery Plays, was obviously being put to good use. As the royal procession moved through the city they were sprinkled with a 'rain of rose water', pelted with hailstones of comfit (a type of sweetmeat) and in Stonegate King Henry was blessed by the Virgin Mary who then ascended into heaven with angels' song whilst wafers were showered onto his courtiers.

Despite this humble submission, the corporation fiercely guarded its own independence from royal interference. An ongoing dispute ensued between the king and corporation about who should fill the important position of 'Recorder'. By playing a delaying game the corporation succeeded in rejecting Henry's choice and eventually chose a former servant of Richard III.

Richard wasn't forgotten by the people of York either. Although evidence is fragmentary, one account does show that in 1491 two drunken men fought over Richard's reputation, and presumably Richard was a favourite topic of conversation after Bosworth in the ale houses and taverns of York.

Henry VIII (1509–1547)

When Henry VIII succeeded to the throne after the death of his father Henry VII no one could have foreseen the massive religious and social changes that would sweep England in his lifetime. A key issue which came to dominate Henry's life was that of his marriage to Catherine of Aragon. Catherine's first marriage was to Henry's older brother, Arthur, who had died in 1502. To continue the political alliance between England and Spain, King Henry VII arranged for his younger son, Henry, to marry Catherine. During the early years of Henry's reign the marriage was a happy one, and Catherine gave birth to a daughter, Mary. However, the continuing lack of a male heir caused Henry to seek a wife who could give him a son. His roving eye fell upon Anne Boleyn. At the same time as Henry was courting Anne, a new religious system of belief was also beginning to percolate from Europe into England: Protestantism.

Protestantism and the Religious Reformation

During the early part of the sixteenth century there were new religious ideas circulating throughout Europe, which were formulated through the potentially revolutionary teachings of theologians such as Martin Luther. The followers of Luther and others were protesting against many of the beliefs and practices of the Catholic church and became known as Protestants.

There are many differences between Catholicism and Protestantism. Some of the most important stem from who has religious authority: Catholics believe in the authority of the Pope and church tradition, whilst Protestants primarily believe in the authority of the Bible above all else.

At the same time as the new Protestant theology was emerging there was also a growing resentment against the wealth, power and corruption within the Catholic church. This anti-clericalism usually took the form of disparaging talk about priests and the Catholic church, though it could also be a refusal to pay church taxes. A person who received vehement criticism was Cardinal Wolsey (1472-1530), Lord Chancellor, and from 1514, archbishop of York. For years Wolsey practically ruled the kingdom, had an income of £50,000 and built three palaces for himself, the most famous being Hampton Court. Wolsey even had plans to become Pope. Wolsey eventually fell out of favour with Henry and fled north to York. He was forcibly recalled to London, but died on the journey south at Nottingham in 1530.

For historians the two strands of the new Protestant beliefs and the age old anti-clericalism have caused many problems. If a person verbally or physically attacked a priest, was it the priest's character he disliked, or the priest's beliefs?

With the religious situation growing increasingly violent on the Continent, the Catholic church in England became ever more strict in hunting out heretics – those people who deliberately did not follow Church teaching and would not change their views. Owing to the Continental connections of immigrants into York the church authorities may have paid them particular attention, and it is noticeable that an early heretic in 1528 was Gilbert Johnson a 'Dutchman and carver'. As a penance he was made to go on four long processions of penance around the city for his anti-Catholic beliefs. A few years later the sons of Frederick Freez, a Dutch printer who lived in York, were arrested as heretics. Edward Freez was imprisoned and died in the Tower of

London. In 1540 Edward's brother, Valentine, and Valentine's wife were burnt for heresy. Valentine was a Freeman of the city and in the Freeman's Register there is a note against his name in Latin 'he was burnt at the Knavesmire on account of heresy'.

THE POLITICAL REFORMATION

Even though there was a growing number of people who were converted to Protestant beliefs, it was King Henry VIII's political situation that was to have the most dramatic impact on English religious life. King Henry was desperate for a son and therefore sought to divorce his queen, Catherine of Aragon, and marry Anne Boleyn. Unfortunately for Henry, divorce was forbidden by the Catholic church, except in extreme circumstances. Henry put increasing pressure on the Pope to grant him a divorce, which included cutting off Papal revenue from England and ultimately Henry declared himself 'as far as the law of Christ allows, supreme head of the Church of England'. In 1532 it was discovered that Anne was with child and in order for the hoped for boy to be born in wedlock Henry and Anne married in January 1533 – even though Henry had not yet divorced Catherine of Aragon. (Henry and Catherine were officially divorced in May.)

The outcome of the divorce was that Henry was excommunicated by the Pope. The irony was that Henry's theology remained largely Catholic. However, England now stood alone against some of the most powerful countries in Europe. Charles V of Spain was Catherine's nephew, and allied to him were the Pope and the French king. Fearful of an invasion and with an empty treasury – as well as a luxuriant lifestyle – Henry needed money fast.

THE DISSOLUTION OF THE SMALLER MONASTERIES 1536

As Henry searched for new sources of wealth he realised that the monasteries not only owned huge estates, but also large amounts of gold, silver and other treasure. In order to help his cause in 1535 church commissioners were sent to the monasteries to seek out 'manifest sin, vicious carnal and abominable living'. The commissioners did their duties well and discovered a vast range of abuse, misconduct and irreligious conduct, all of which was carefully recorded. However, whilst there was undoubtedly some abuse of the system, it is highly likely that the commissioners embellished their findings to help the king's cause. In the summer of 1536 an Act of Parliament was passed to close, or 'dissolve' all religious houses having an income of less than £200 a year. The first religious house in York to be closed was the small nunnery of St Clement's, just outside the city walls, on 31 August 1536.

THE PILGRIMAGE OF GRACE, OCTOBER 1536

The Pilgrimage of Grace was the greatest northern rebellion of the Tudor age. It had many causes, economic, social and agricultural, but the rebels united under the cause of religion. They wanted a return to the old ways and whilst supporting Henry VIII wanted the policies to change. The leader was Robert Aske, a gentleman who lived just outside York at Aughton.

Aske harnessed the existing resentment against the religious and social changes that were happening in the north. One particularly hated change was the enclosing of land, whereby lands owned by a group of people were fenced and henceforward owned by a single person. Within York the citizens had previously rioted because of new enclosures which had fenced off common land. Physical violence had been used to tear down the fences and two women were punished for putting a curse on the mayor – their punishment was to be carted round the city for three days.

The people, or 'commons' as they were known at the time, were restive and the ruling authorities were fearful. On 10 October people in York heard of Aske's rising and the next day a group of rebels appeared before the gates of the city. Fuel was poured onto the flames by letters circulating suggesting that the king was about to close churches as well as tax marriages and christenings – all untrue but useful to anger the population.

With the situation becoming out of hand the king's main councillors in York, including the Archbishop Lee, fled to the safety of Pontefract twenty miles south on 13 October. The stakes were further raised when the main force of rebels appeared before the gates of the city. The estimates as to how large the force was varied, ranging between 20,000 and 40,000 men, but even the lowest estimate was a substantial number of men.

The next day, 16 October, Aske with 4,000 to 5,000 horsemen entered the city, though the foot soldiers were required to stay outside – having a horse indicated status and by association honour, whereas foot soldiers had a reputation for looting. Not only was there no resistance, Aske and the other leaders were received at the door of the Minster and then processed to the high altar. The city had been taken for rebel cause.

Aske left the city on the 18th with a forward group and headed south and two days later the main force left. On leaving the rebels held a procession through York at which the Abbot of St Mary's Abbey reluctantly carried his finest cross at the head of the procession. He was obviously uncomfortable in this role and left as soon as possible.

Within a few months the rebellion had collapsed. Aske and the other leaders were declared traitors, tortured and beheaded. The most influential York churchman to receive this fate was John Pickering, the Prior of the Dominican Friary on Toft Green. He was captured and sent to the Tower of London, condemned for treason and executed on 27 May 1537. Aske had a more local death and in July was hanged at York Castle.

THE DISSOLUTION OF THE MONASTERIES CONTINUES 1539

Following the defeat of the Pilgrimage of Grace, combined with Henry's joint desire for religious change and money, the spoliation of the churches continued. In 1538 the shrines of saints were destroyed, their valuables being graciously received by the king, and secondly in 1539 the larger, wealthier religious houses were dissolved. During the Middle Ages York had a substantial number of churches and the dissolution of 1539 included the closure of St Mary's Abbey, the Dominican, Fransciscan, Carmelite and Augustinian friaries, and St Andrew's Gilbertine Priory. As well as the monasteries and friaries, other religious houses were closed, notably St Leonard's Hospital, the largest hospital in the north of England. Even York Minster was not immune and church property passed from the church into lay hands.

The graceful ruins of St Mary's Abbey

Within the space of a few years the religious landscape of York had changed forever.

The richer members of society bought up the lands and buildings of the monasteries and either converted them into palatial residences for themselves, or sold the lead, stone and other materials to make a profit. Thus some buildings were looted and disappeared entirely, whilst some were adapted and remained. St Mary's Abbey – the largest Benedictine monastery in the north – was partly robbed and allowed to fall into disrepair and was partly converted into an elegant residence. Today the ruined church stands as a beautiful reminder of former elegance, whilst the Abbot's lodging has survived as King's Manor and is today part of the University of York.

HENRY VIII'S VISIT, 1541

The potential consequences of the authorities in York allowing entry to the rebels of the Pilgrimage of Grace resulted in them once again being very fearful of a king's visit. The Corporation made a grovelling submission to the king when Henry VIII visited the city in person in 1541. There was considerable apprehension in the city for the king could have taken what revenge he liked. The most important men fell to their knees on his approach and declared that by odious offence and traitorous rebellion they had heinously offended the king. Just in case their submission and words were not enough they presented to the king a cup filled with £100 of gold, and to Henry's queen they gave a cup containing £40 of gold.

Before Henry VIII's visit, York had consistently been on the opposing side to the Tudor monarchy, whether by supporting Richard III against Henry VII or during the Pilgrimage of Grace. Henry VIII's stay marked a turning point and from that time onwards York stood behind the Tudors, and indeed the legitimate monarchs thereafter.

Edward VI (1547–1553)

Henry VIII died in 1547 and his young son was crowned king as Edward VI. (The numbering, 'VI', was further Tudor propaganda against Richard III who, it was alleged, had killed his nephew, the rightful King Edward V.)

Edward and his advisers, the Protectors Somerset and Northumberland, drove the country in an increasingly hardline Protestant direction, a policy which had profound effects upon the beliefs of the Church of England.

THE CLOSURE OF THE CHANTRIES AND RELIGIOUS GUILDS 1546–7

The reign of Henry VIII had seen sweeping changes by the closure of the monasteries and friaries, but Henry's changes were as much about seizing wealth as a radical change in theology. However, under his son Edward VI traditional Catholic beliefs and practices were attacked.

In 1546 and 1547 the pace of the Reformation quickened as religious revenues of religious guilds, hospitals and chantries were directed into the crown's coffers. (A chantry was an altar at which a priest prayed for a single person or family.) Without money the institutions folded. The presence of the religious guilds and chantries had been an integral part of religious life for centuries. The single largest group of chantries were in the Minster, where forty-seven chantries were served by forty-nine priests. A further forty-one chantries were spread between the other nineteen churches in the city. Twelve guilds were suppressed, the most important of which was the Corpus Christi Guild. At the height of its power in the previous century it included amongst its members Richard III and his relatives, archbishops of York, noblemen, abbots and city dignitaries. Over its 140 years in existence nearly 17,000 people joined the Guild.

The most visible change was to the look of churches as the reformers ordered the stripping out of items that had been given to, or acquired by, churches over the centuries. The most dramatic was the removal of the Minster's relics and precious objects. A list has survived of the Minster's possessions, including: the Rod of Aaron; some Manna from heaven which fed the Israelites; stones that had been sat on by John the Baptist, the Angel at the tomb and Christ whilst he was fasting; hair of St William; six heads of saints and three arms; five teeth and three phials of blood, as well as thirty saints' bones. The Minster also had numerous gold and silver crosses, chalices and patens, shrines and vestments. Whilst undoubtedly being poorer materially, by sweeping away such items the reformers aimed to lessen the distractions within church so that worshippers could hear the Word of God single-mindedly.

York's Economic Decline Continues

Since the peak of York's prosperity in the thirteenth and fourteenth centuries York had slowly declined economically, with a marked decline being experienced in the Tudor period. The authorities were well aware of the situation and wrote to influential people to try and gain help. In reply to a plea to repair the castle and walls, King Henry VII wrote that in the city there were many 'placs [places] and parisches theroff is fallen into suche extreme ruyne and decaye'. The same theme was echoed later in the sixteenth century, with properties in 1562 being described as in 'ruyne and decaye' and nearly forty years later in 1598 the city was described as enduring 'great ruin and long decay'.

The reasons for the decay of the once noble city were known to contemporaries. The strict rules and laws of the city, and especially the trade guilds, had meant that groups of traders had left the city to less regulated areas, whether in the countryside or the newly emerging towns of the West Riding of Yorkshire, such as Leeds, Halifax and

Wakefield. This was especially true of the textile industry where the West Riding towns could produce more cloth and thereby took trade from York. The few textile workers remaining in York had looms 'which for the most part doo stand unoccupied for lak of work'.

Other reasons for York's decline included the deteriorating condition of the River Ouse as a river for trade, which in turn hindered international commerce. The tidal nature of the River Ouse had also led to the port of Hull at the mouth of the River Humber becoming the transhipment departure point of choice for Yorkshire and foreign merchants.

A further reason for the decline may have been the closure of the religious houses and the impact of the Reformation, though the actual impact is difficult to quantify. The monasteries in particular had been centres of wealth creation through the selling of wool and many monasteries through Yorkshire had houses in York. However, it is debatable how much the closure of the monasteries affected York's prosperity, because with their closure large amounts of land passed into lay hands and noblemen or the wealthier citizens bought up property thereby potentially stimulating the economy. King's Manor, the former lodging of the abbot of St Mary's Abbey became the seat of the King's Council of the North.

Despite the economic problems, by the end of the century the financial fortunes of the city had gradually begun to revive as the guild restrictions were slowly relaxed and in the following century York became a favoured destination of the wealthy gentry of the county.

Queen Mary (1553–1558)

Following Edward VI's death there was a brief attempt to secure the monarchy for a Protestant monarch and Edward's 'protector' Northumberland married his son to a distant claimant to the throne, Lady Jane Grey. The scheme had no support and quickly collapsed. Although never crowned, Lady Jane Gray became known as the 'Nine Days Queen'. Unfortunately she paid the price for her father in law's political deviousness and, although merely a political puppet, she was later executed.

The queen who was crowned was Mary Tudor, the eldest child of Henry VIII, whose mother was Catherine of Aragon. Mary was a devoted Catholic and whereas the church in England had lurched towards more extreme Protestantism under Edward VI, Mary moved the church towards Catholicism. Mary attempted to undo many of the changes that had occurred under her father, Henry VIII, and half-brother Edward. The Mass and other former services were revived, and priests were required to be celibate once more: those who married under Henry and Edward now had the awful choice of their wife or their religious vocation. However, despite Mary's desire, the monasteries or friaries could not be restored because their lands had been sold off.

As Mary's policies reinstated Catholic beliefs, items previously banned, such as vestments and religious items, were brought back into religious services. There was, however, no widespread and spontaneous enthusiasm for the revival of Catholic practices by the people of York and amongst the clergy of the Minster there was a cautious and hesitant approach to the religious reforms.

Queen Mary ruled for five years during which the church had veered back towards Catholicism. Mary had also reforged alliances with Catholic countries and had married the powerful Catholic king, King Philip II of Spain. However, her life ended in tragedy, with a husband who avoided her, a people only partially accepting her religious changes and a pregnancy which was not a longed-for child, but dropsy, a medical condition which eventually killed her.

Elizabeth I (1558–1603)

The day on which Elizabeth came to the throne was treated as a national holiday for two centuries afterwards. Queen Elizabeth's view of religious belief was studiously neutral and she famously said that she would not 'make windows into men's souls'. This was probably a relief to the majority of the population as the previous monarchs had swung between extreme Protestantism and Catholicism. However, whilst Elizabeth might not have been that interested, the authorities nationally and within York promoted Protestantism. This was reflected in the changing culture of the city in the following decades.

A CHANGE IN CULTURE 1560–1580

During the religious turmoil of the previous decades, many of the city's traditions had continued. However, thirty years after the first changes of the Reformation the increasingly strict reformers sought to improve church attendance by decree. In 1588 orders were given that shops and doors must be closed while church sermons and services were taking place. They also began to re-evaluate the old customs of York and either ban them or adapt them.

One custom which was banned was that of the riding of Yule and Yule's Wife through the city. The riders were disguised and rode in a very 'indecent and uncomely manner' which resulted in a large crowd gathering who themselves committed other (unspecified) enormities. Other activities banned included performances by the Lords of Misrule at Christmas or at the May games, Morris dancers or minstrels. Even the Mystery Plays were either reformed or banned.

The reasons behind these changes were twofold. The first was that the reformers genuinely wanted to lessen obscenity and increase decorum and moral attitudes. The second reason was that there was a serious concern that boisterous behaviour by the crowds would lead to riots and threaten the stability of the city. The religious and social changes of the previous half century, as well as economic depression and increasing number of beggars, had created a great unease amongst the city authorities who wanted to lessen the opportunities for rioting.

BEGGARS AND VAGRANCY

Even though York's economy was not particularly prosperous, the city was a magnet for the poverty stricken from rural areas. Increasing vagrancy was a problem common to most towns in the sixteenth century as agricultural practices changed. In the countryside the practice of amalgamating small farming plots and arable strips into a single bigger unit owned by one person (a practice known as enclosure) meant that many people were driven from the land.

As the number of beggars swelled in York, the corporation took action to distinguish those who could not work and had no other means of support and those who begged because they were too lazy to do anything else. From 1515 legal beggars were obliged to wear tokens on their shoulders, and those without would be expelled from the city. In 1528 a hierarchy of beggars was instigated, whereby a 'Master Beggar' was appointed for each ward, or administrative district, who checked on the other beggars. Any who arrived and did not have a token was required to leave as soon as possible.

The Justices of the Peace also had a role to play and as well as emphasising virtues they could use whipping to cajole beggars to work. They also had wider powers and could examine suspicious strangers, uphold statutes against gaming, bowling and illegal tippling houses, and enforce curfews.

Margaret Clitheroe – Catholic Martyr 1586

Margaret Clitheroe is York's only Catholic saint from the sixteenth century. She was born in York in 1553 as Margaret Middleton. Her father was a prominent York citizen, being sheriff and also church warden of St Martin's in Coney Street. After his death his widow married again, to Henry May, who himself rose to become Lord Mayor of the city in 1586. Margaret therefore came from a well-to-do family with extensive connections within York. At the age of fifteen she married a wealthy butcher, John Clitheroe. There was nothing in her early life to mark her out as a person of intense faith. However, during the 1570s she became increasingly strong in her Catholic faith, a factor which must have made her husband's life very difficult as he was responsible for reporting Catholic worshippers to the Protestant authorities in the parish.

Margaret was constantly put in prison for her Catholic beliefs. Her first short imprisonment was in 1577, but after her release she continued to help and support other Catholics in York. The pattern of imprisonment and then Margaret continuing her actions repeated itself through the rest of her life. During the 1580s her house in the Shambles became the main focus for Catholic religion in a country and city where it was illegal. In two years, 1582 and 1583, five Catholic priests were captured in Yorkshire, tried and then hung on the gallows at Tyburn. Margaret visited the gallows at night, kneeling and praying at the site of their death. She created a secret room within her house as a refuge for Catholic priests.

The York authorities were growing increasingly alarmed about Margaret's activities. A lightning raid upon her house resulted in a boy telling of the secret room. Margaret was tried for harbouring priests, the penalty for which was death by hanging. At her trial Margaret stubbornly refused to say the words necessary to start the proceedings. This left the judge in a dilemma, so warning her of a 'sharp death' he delayed proceedings to allow her to consider her options. The authorities over the previous decades had constantly sought to change Margaret's views, but their attempts and the final delay were to no avail. The judge reluctantly declared she should be put to death by being crushed under heavy weights, a punishment which was carried out on 25 March 1586.

Margaret Clitheroe was not forgotten and in 1929 she was beatified and then in 1970 she was canonised by the Pope. A house in the Shambles is today a shrine to her memory.

AN OPINION OF ELIZABETHAN YORK, 1589

In 1589 James Ryther, the owner of Harewood House, sent an acerbic report about York to Lord Burghley, one of Queen Elizabeth's most important ministers. There are few descriptions of York before the seventeenth century and this one highlighted some less than legal practices by merchants and tradesmen. Ryther stated that the richer merchants sold products bought cheaply from London at an extortionate price and lent money at usurous rates, therefore making many men poorer. Ryther was also scathing about the skills of the craftsmen or tradesmen ('artificers' he calls them) and reported that even though there are many of them, they were unskilled and sold things too expensively. Leisure time too came under the spotlight and he was disgusted by the ale, which he described as 'not good nor wholesome. Their ale ... is mingled with resin to make it strong, in some parts with urine'.

Ryther's final comments described a city in some decay, with the castle ruinous, the city altered (probably from the destruction at the Reformation) and numerous churches which were so decayed that there were gardens and orchards within their precincts. One oddity to a modern reader is that he describes the Minster as 'but a new building'.

The King's Council of the North

During the Middle Ages York had briefly been the capital of England during the Scottish Wars and, although it never regained this title, the city during the Tudor period became the capital of northern England by the presence of the King's Council of the North. This body had originally been set up by Richard III, but it was following the Pilgrimage of Grace in 1536 until the end of the century, that the Council had its greatest power. The Council had numerous roles, but one of the most difficult was making sure the authorities of the towns of the north compiled with national legislation. As the Council was based in York, the York mayor and corporation were often in the firing line with firm reminders to enforce various laws. In 1577 the Council required the York Corporation to enforce the statutes forbidding the eating of flesh in Lent, and unlawful games, as well as to prevent riots and unlawful gatherings.

By the beginning of the next century the Council of the North had lost some of its power because its role had changed. During the last half of the sixteenth century it was primarily, and effectively, in charge of the administration of the region, but as the seventeenth century progressed the Council was involved in more and more legal cases. In effect it became a court run by lawyers and therefore the Council lost much of its administrative power.

James I (1603–1625)

On 24 March 1603 Elizabeth I died and with her ended the tumultuous Tudor dynasty. As Elizabeth was unmarried and childless the succession of the kingdom passed to James VI of Scotland (who became James I of England) whose great, great grandfather was Henry VII. The succession resulted in the joining of the crowns of England and Scotland.

York became a focus for the preparations, both for James I's journey south from Scotland and to keep law and order in the north. Both tasks were given to the Council of the North to organise and oversee. In 1599 Thomas Cecil, second Lord Burghley, one of Elizabeth's most trusted advisers, was appointed Lord President of the Council of the North.

The news of the queen's death reached York on 27 March. Two proclamations were read by members of the Council of the North and the mayor and corporation – one at Pavement and the other at the south door of the Minster.

James himself arrived in York on Saturday 16 April and the following day was given a silver gilt cup and money by the mayor, to which he replied 'God will bless you better, for your goodwill towards your King'. The king left the city on the following Monday, first having processed through the city to the cheering crowds. The visit had been very successful and the extensive planning and tight security resulted in both peace in the north and James safely travelling down from Scotland to London to be crowned.

GUY FAWKES AND THE GUNPOWDER PLOT

Guy Fawkes, who was born in York, gained his notoriety and infamy through his central role in the Gunpowder Plot. Guy Fawkes was baptised at St Michael Le Belfry on 13 April 1570, though the location of his birth is disputed and two nearby establishments claim that he was born in their premises.

Guy's father, Edward, was a Protestant, and was an influential figure in York. However, he died in 1578 when Guy was only eight years old. His mother remarried and the family moved out of York to the nearby village of Scotton. Guy had a good schooling and attended St Peter's School (then located at the end of Gillygate). With him were the brothers John and Christopher Wright, who also were involved in the Gunpowder Plot.

When Guy came of age he moved back to York and acquired land in Clifton and Gillygate. Even though he could have lived a comfortable life in York, Guy began to mix with Catholics and he and his cousin, Harrington, journeyed to Flanders. In Flanders his cousin Harrington became a Catholic priest and Guy enlisted in the Catholic Spanish army and commanded a unit of soldiers. His military service brought him to the attention of the Spanish authorities and he was sent to 'enlighten King Philip II of Spain concerning the true position of [Roman Catholics] in England'.

Whilst in Europe Guy became part of a group of conspirators who planned to blow up the Houses of Parliament whilst King James was opening it. The plan involved igniting barrels of gunpowder placed in the cellars. However, Parliament also included some Catholic lords and so to warn them a letter was sent to Lord Monteagle, who was himself a Catholic. Monteagle passed the letter straight on to William Cecil, King James's Secretary of State. In ignorance of the discovery of the plot the preparations continued. It was Guy Fawkes's duty to guard the cellar and light the gunpowder whilst the other plotters would rally the Catholics of England to fight for their cause. After lighting the gun-powder Guy Fawkes's mission was to raise forces in Flanders for the invasion of England.

It took the authorities two searches on successive nights to discover Guy Fawkes and the gunpowder. The full scale of the plot was quickly revealed and the other conspirators were hunted down. Guy Fawkes was eventually put to death by the grisly method of hanging, drawing and quartering – a terrible death reserved for the worst of traitors.

Mapping the City

The first map of York survives as an portion of a larger ink-lined map of the city centre. The map is undated but it is thought to have been from around 1545 and contains some features, such as the church of St Peter the Little, which was soon after demolished. The first full map of York was drawn by the cartographer John Speed as part of a larger work which mapped Britain and the main towns. Speed's maps were considered to be the most accurate for the time and set a high standard for others to follow. The map of York shows many interesting features such as swans swimming on the King's Fishpool, Clifford's Tower with a roof on (the roof was destroyed in 1684), and numerous windmills in the fields surrounding the city. Thereafter there were an increasing number of maps drawn and Archer's map of 1680 shows not only a Civil War gun emplacement on the Mount, but also individual plots of land in the city.

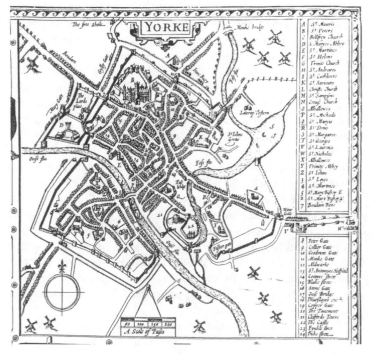

John Speed's map of York in 1611

A Great Family – the Ingrams

The sixteenth and seventeenth centuries continued to see a number of great families dominating national and regional politics and the presence of many of them was also felt in York. There were many who lived in Yorkshire, such as the Wentworths, Scropes and Maleverers and the Fairfax family who also owned property in York. All played varying parts in the history of the nation and region and it was Ferdinando Fairfax who commanded the Parliamentarian forces during the Civil War siege of York. However, one of the families which had the greatest impact upon York in the seventeenth century was the Ingram family.

The family owned impressive estates in Yorkshire and the north. Sir

Arthur Ingram first became known in York in 1613 when he became the Secretary of the Council of the North. Ingram had made his fortune as a merchant and acquired over forty manors and estates in Yorkshire which gave him at his death in 1642 an income of *c.* £10,000 a year. He acquired the Archbishop's Palace which was described as 'utterly ruinous waste' with 'boggs and wattery marrish ground so that the same was altogether unfitt for habitation'. From this desolate spot behind the Minster Ingram built a magnificent mansion with a bowling green, tennis court and fishponds. The mansion was also a symbol of status, wealth and honour.

In 1641 King Charles I visited the house. Sir Arthur Ingram was elsewhere, but his wife, Lady Mary, was hostess for a great feast. Like the house, the meal was a fabulous one and designed to impress with 2000 oysters, four fat turkeys, eight chickens, forty-five partridges, thirty-six teal, twenty-four plovers, six pheasants and 360 pheasant eggs and twelve mallards and snipe. The king stayed for a week – which incurred expenses of £98 1s 7d. Six extra cooks were employed and labourers carried in peat for the cooking ovens. Fortunately the week was a great success and the king, princes and lords were 'infinitely pleased with their entertainment'.

The Ingram family also built Temple Newsam near Leeds which still remains as a magnificent stately home. Gradually Temple Newsam became the favoured home of the family and their York mansion fell into decay. It was entirely demolished by 1830 and is one of the great buildings of York to have disappeared without a trace.

It is ironic that the only building which survives that was funded by the Ingram's family is also one of the smallest that they built – a series of almshouses on Bootham constructed between 1630 and 1632. Included within them, and facing the street, is a Norman doorway, brought from the church of Holy Trinity Micklegate in 1630.

Charles I (1625–1649)

During the reign of Charles I the country was torn apart by the greatest civil war in English history. There is still great debate about the causes of the war, with some historians citing the crown's disputes with

Parliament whilst others describe the tensions between Charles's Catholic supporters and the more Protestant members of Parliament and merchant class.

TENSION MOUNTS

During the 1630s and 1640s the divisions between King Charles and the Parliamentary leaders became wider. Key issues included the right of the king to tax the population, and the differences of religious beliefs. Within York, religion was the divisive issue during the 1630s and 1640s. During the late sixteenth and early seventeenth century, Puritan preachers, who were ultra Protestant in their religious beliefs, had been welcomed by both the archbishops of York and the city authorities. Sermons were a popular way of spreading the message and the city corporation paid for preachers to exhort the population to live a religious life. The joint liaison between the archbishops and the city came to an abrupt end with the death of Archbishop Matthew in 1628. The following archbishops were very different. They belonged to the Arminian tradition which believed that religious worship was heightened by the presence of beautiful and ornate churches, as well as bells, candles and incense during services. This attitude was in direct contrast to the Puritan view that such things detracted from worship and that what was important was that people should fully concentrate on the Word by listening to sermons without any distractions.

York was not alone in this division of religious opinions and it was a debate which caused fundamental disagreements across England. The city authorities responded by paying for the livings of two churches, All Saint's Pavement and St Saviours in 1632. The emphasis put upon the sermon, and hence the Word of God, can still be seen today in All Saint's Pavement where the eye is drawn to the large three-decker pulpit from which the sermon is still delivered every Sunday. From this high vantage point the preacher looks down upon the congregation and can easily spot if anyone is not paying attention.

TWO ROYAL VISITS 1633 AND 1642

Kings only occasionally visited York and they were usually warmly welcomed. Charles's visit of 1633, however, had a different tone.

Whilst the city authorities were not openly hostile to the king, they favoured Puritanism whilst King Charles supported the Arminian tradition and when he visited York he actively helped the Minster authorities, donating £1000 to provide beautiful items for the church, such as altar cloths, an organ and a new brightly gilded altar screen.

Charles I's second visit to York in 1642 was forced upon him as opposition to his rule had grown so vociferous in London that he fled north. Charles stayed in the city with his family for six months. Whilst Charles was in the north, London and the south-east was ruled by Parliament. In order to increase his military support in the city Charles held two musters of the militia, first at the Castle (the traditional location for such occasions) and then at Heworth Moor. Meanwhile the king's supporters had also been increasing the output of royal propaganda and a Royalist press printed pamphlets from St William's College.

In the city the corporation was in a very awkward position. Some of the council's members were Puritan sympathisers and stayed away from council meetings and in the town Puritan preachers could still command eager listeners. However, apart from attempting to keep the peace – not always successfully – there was not a lot the council could do to promote Puritan views with the forceful presence of the king and his entourage in the city.

As the situation worsened nationally the king began to take military action, and his first act was an unsuccessful raid on Beverley. A few weeks later the king marched south out of York and formally raised his standard at Nottingham. The Civil War had started.

The Civil War

For eighteen months there was something of a phoney war with preparations for battle but little real fighting nearby. Royalist troops were billeted in the town but as they had no money they could not pay for their food or accommodation. The corporation appeal to the supreme commander of the Royalist forces, the marquis of Newcastle, for additional funds was unsuccessful.

As well as refusing funds, the marquis insisted that a Royalist supporter, Edmund Cowper, was elected mayor. This interference was bitterly resented, even by councillors with Royalist sympathies, but there was little they could do. The visit to the city in 1643 by the Catholic queen, Henrietta Maria, did nothing to calm the passions which were running high in the city.

THE SIEGE OF YORK

By the autumn of 1643 the Royalists were still in the ascendant but were slowly losing ground to the increasingly powerful Parliamentarian army. The north of England had generally supported Charles I, though the larger mercantile cities such as Hull and Manchester were outposts of Parliamentarian support. To the north of York however were the Royalist strongholds of Newcastle and Durham.

By 1644 Charles and Parliament had reached a stalemate and both looked for allies beyond England. Charles raised Catholic troops in Ireland, whilst Parliament secured the support of the powerful Scottish army. The Scots slowly worked their way southwards, but their journey had been slowed by bad weather conditions and stubborn resistance.

York's strategic location suddenly became a major determining factor of the war. A Royalist force from York could march north, defeat the Scots and secure the north of England for the king. However, if the Royalist garrison in York could be defeated, then northern support for King Charles would crumble. A Parliamentary army moved north under the command of Ferdinando, second Baron Fairfax. His job was to contain the sizeable York garrison of some 4000 men.

As Fairfax's army moved north a letter fell into the hands of the York commander John Bellasis which potentially revolutionised the situation, because the letter revealed the detailed plans of Ferdinando Fairfax. Fairfax's plan was to unite his scattered forces at Selby before besieging York. Acting on this remarkable information Bellasis marched from York with a large contingent of 3000 troops to Selby. It was a pivotal moment in control of the north, for in the ensuing fighting Bellasis was taken prisoner and contemporary reports indicated that up to 2000 Royalist soldiers were killed or captured. It was a stunning

Ferdinando Fairfax, the commander of the Parliamentarian forces in the
Civil War

Parliamentary victory which shifted the balance of power from the
Royalists to the Parliamentarian side.

York had since Roman times always been a military strongpoint and
during the earlier stages of the Civil War had begun to build up its
fortifications. The main point of defence was the castle, though Clifford's Tower was largely ruinous. The city walls were repaired and
small towers were built on the walls to further strengthen the defences.
One proposed defensive measure which was not fulfilled was the
destruction of the houses and buildings built against and near the city
walls to a depth of 'twenty-five score paces'. This defensive measure
was a practical and sensible one because the buildings could afford
cover for an attacking force, but not unnaturally the home owners and
merchants objected. The marquis of Newcastle, garrisoned in York,
also had several concerns as he had not enough provisions for his troops
and the cavalry, and if a siege ensued it would be tying up fighting men
who could better help the king's cause elsewhere. For this reason he

dispatched his best cavalry out of the city to join the king's forces in the Midlands.

Following the Parliamentarian victory at Selby the Parliamentarian soldiers and the Scottish army, which had moved south, finally joined together into a formidable fighting force. However, even the combined force was not strong enough to take the strongly fortified city of York. Whilst they waited for the third, larger and better equipped Parliamentarian force led by the earl of Manchester to journey from Lincoln the besiegers could only throw a cordon around the city. By Monday 27 May the earl of Manchester had personally met the other commanders with his army close behind. Manchester and his forces made their way round to the north side of the city (in the Clifton area) and made a bridge by tying boats together so that his army and the Scots army were linked together.

The net was now tightening around York, and Fairfax's Parliamentarian forces built a battery on Lamel Hill, which is now where the Retreat Hospital is situated, to bombard the Walmgate defences. A further battery was created within St Lawrence churchyard, a long stone's throw from Walmgate Bar itself.

The use of cannon played a critical part in the Civil Wars and many of the cannons were named and became famous in their own right. One particularly famous cannon was known as 'The Queen's Pocket-Pistol' and had originally belonged to the marquis of Newcastle, before it was captured at Hull by the Parliamentarian forces and turned against the marquis who was defending York. The next phase of the siege was that of cannon bombardment by both sides.

The steady bombardment by both sides demolished buildings in the vicinity. The steeples of St Denys's church and St Sampson's church in the heart of York were both shot through with cannon balls which had been fired from Lamnel Hill battery.

Around the defences Fairfax's force begun to undermine the walls at Walmgate, but this was discovered and the mine was neutralised. The houses and shops in the suburbs were burnt by the defenders and two bridges, one at Monk Bar and the other at Layerthorpe were also torn down.

The most audacious attack occurred when Manchester's Parliamentarian forces dug a tunnel under St Mary's Tower in Bootham which was then blown up. Unfortunately it was blown up prematurely before all the Parliamentarian troops were ready. (The possible reasons for this being either that the tunnel became flooded, or that a certain Colonel Crawford wanted the glory of the action for himself). The attack was repulsed after heavy fighting and the attackers pushed back, but the defenders blocked their exist, with the result that over two hundred Parliamentarian soldiers were captured. What could have been a well-planned and executed triumph for the Parliamentarian forces had turned into a chaotic rout.

The mining and blowing up of St Mary's Tower has had a much longer impact upon the writing of York's history, for in the tower were large amounts of records relating to St Mary's Abbey. It is fortunate that many had been copied a few years in 1635–6 by the antiquarian Robert Dodsworth. His unique records now reside in the Bodleian Library in Oxford. After the dust had settled the documents that could be recovered were retrieved. One of these was one of the three surviving cartularies (books of charter records) of St Mary's Abbey which today is one of the glories of York Minster Library.

THE ARRIVAL OF THE ROYALIST ARMY

The failure of the attack and increasing sickness were two reasons for the sagging confidence of the Parliamentarian forces, but there was another, greater, anxiety. The Royalist army, led by the dashing Prince Rupert, was rumoured to be heading north to relieve York, which in turn caused a rise in confidence amongst the besieged in the city. However, accurate news was very difficult to obtain by the besieged as the Parliamentarian forces encircling the city had cut off all Royalist movement to the world beyond. One method the Royalists in York had of signalling to Prince Rupert was by burning fires on top of the Minster.

However, instead of a direct assault from the west, Prince Rupert's troops marched to the north, crossing the River Ouse at Borough-bridge and then marched down the Ouse into the Clifton area, the area where Manchester's troops had been. The Parliamentarian forces had been deceived by Rupert's manoeuvre and believing that the Royalist area would attack in the west, had concentrated their forces around Long Marston. The attackers positions were deserted and in the Walmgate sector one of the Royalist defenders had left the city to see 'what became of ye enemy'. The positions were quite deserted and the huts empty. The siege had been lifted and the Royalist defenders joyously welcomed Prince Rupert's army. Though Prince Rupert did not enter the city himself, there was constant communication between the Royalist commanders.

THE BATTLE OF MARSTON MOOR, 1642

The Parliamentarian forces had been out-manoeuvred by Prince Rupert, and were still unsure where his army was, so Rupert decided to take advantage of the element of surprise. He marched to Marston Moor and, on 2 July 1642, caught the Parliamentarian troops stretched out from Long Marston to Tadcaster. The Royalist army had the strong advantage, but Rupert did not press home the attack and waited for the other elements of his army to join him. As time wore on his advantage withered away as the Parliamentarian forces regrouped. The forces that Rupert waited for were the marquis of Newcastle's troops in York. The marquis had thought himself slighted by Rupert and was therefore very reluctant to join Rupert's troops. The garrison troops eventually arrived at Marston Moor at four o'clock in the afternoon. By the time both sides were in position it was late in the afternoon and various Royalist commanders, including Prince Rupert and Newcastle, left the field thinking it was too late to start fighting. The numerically stronger Parliamentarian forces therefore took the Royalists completely by surprise as they advanced – between 6 and 7 o'clock in the evening. As dusk fell the battle scene was illuminated by a full harvest moon.

The cavalry charged first, the outcome of which was Prince Rupert's Royalist cavalry were routed – the first occurrence during the war. The other Royalist cavalry unit was more successful, though they chased the Parliamentarian soldiers and discovered the Parliamentarian baggage train, which occupied them rather than returning to the fray. Both sides suffered considerable casualties, and in the end it was the Parliamentarian cavalry led by Oliver Cromwell (who was rapidly rising up the ranks) that in combination with the foot soldiers crushed the Royalist army. The result was a resounding success for the Parliamentarian forces.

Prince Rupert survived and made his way to the city by 11 o'clock at night. Many other Royalists also straggled into city during the hours after the battle, for York still offered significant defences.

The Royalist commanders decided to quickly leave York. Rupert and a small cavalry headed north, whilst the marquis of Newcastle and some twenty-two other commanders travelled to Scarborough, from there fleeing the country and settling in Hamburg. Newcastle returned in 1660 when Charles II was restored to the throne.

THE RESUMPTION AND END OF THE SIEGE

Two days later, on 4 July, the Parliamentarian forces once again blockaded the city. The siege had resumed. There was some bombardment by cannon and preparations for attack, but it was obvious that the defenders did not have the manpower to defend the city, nor was a Royalist relieving force likely to appear, so the city set about agreeing terms of surrender. By 16 July terms had been agreed and the Royalists marched out of York. They had been granted safe passage to another Royalist garrison town at Skipton, but some soldiers of the Parliamentarian army pillaged the Royalist wagons, until this practice was halted by the Parliamentarian officers.

On entering York the Parliamentarian leaders 'marched with a great traine' to the Minster where a thanksgiving service was held for their victory. For the next sixteen years (until the Restoration of Charles II) the Minster belonged to the citizens of York without interference from the Church of England, a situation which has never occurred before or since. This was made easier by the archbishop fleeing to Wales, and the dean being in a London prison for debt.

THE DAMAGE TO YORK

The damage to York caused by the two sieges was extensive. The most hard-hit areas were the suburbs, in particular those outside Micklegate Bar, Monkgate Bar and Walmgate, though no suburbs completely escaped unscathed. The destruction of these areas resulted in a later building campaign which has left many fine Georgian houses, excellent examples of which can be seen today along Bootham.

Within the walls the high steeples of many of the medieval churches were obvious landmarks for the besiegers to aim for with cannon. However, for the attackers the church steeples were also seen as signs of Catholicism (presumably as they contained bells). As one tract written *c*. 1680 recounted, the Parliamentarian forces could not stomach 'these steeple houses (as they then scornfully termed [them and] ... by their continuall shooting against them and endeavouring to destroy them'. Particular targets were St Sampson's church, which suffered badly from cannon balls shot through its steeple, St Denys's church and St George's church. Both sides also used churches as defensive positions and the tops of towers were ideal platforms for gun batteries. The Royalist forces probably used the top of St Olave's Tower as one such battery and at the other side of York the churches of St Lawrence's church and St Nicholas's church, both outside Walmgate Bar, were used by Parliamentarian forces and were severely damaged by Royalist defenders.

However, despite all the destruction there were some incredible survivals, the greatest of which was the medieval stained glass within the Minster. It was Lord Fairfax who proclaimed that there was to be no ransacking or destruction of York churches, and unlike many other churches the interiors and medieval stained glass survived.

THE PEOPLE OF YORK

The siege was a dreadful ordeal for both attackers and defenders alike, for sickness was rife on both sides. However, the attacking armies were at least able to scavenge for food in the countryside, whilst the defenders were purely reliant on stored provisions.

As was common in the Civil War wives would be part of the armies that their husbands were in. Many women had accompanied their husbands into York, but with the defeat of York the wives wanted to return home. Journeying through the countryside held by Parliamentarian forces was potentially very hazardous, but one way to gain some security was to obtain a safe conduct by one or more of the Parliamentarian generals

But as well as the grim reality of siege, there were one or two lighter moments and narrow escapes. One building, now long demolished was the market house, which stood in Thursday Market (now called St Sampson's Square). A cannon ball, probably shot from Lamel Hill, broke a beam, which caused a couple of dried fish to be cast down on Mistress Clarke 'which knocked her under the Table, being almost fourscore of age, so that the Table did preserve her from hurt'.

Quakers, and Non-conformists

At the start of the Civil War York had strong Royalist sympathies and had been more tolerant of Catholics than more hard line Protestant cities who had supported the Parliamentarian cause. However, with the fall of the city to the Parliamentarian forces and the religious fervour of the country becoming more Protestant, different religious Protestant groups began forming in the city.

In 1651 a preacher by the name of George Fox arrived and was allowed to address the congregation in the Minster, but he verbally attacked the clergy and 'As soon as the words were out of my mouth, they hurried me out, and threw me down the steps. But I got up again without hurt, and went to my lodging, and several were convinced there'. George Fox was the leader of the Society of Friends, or 'Quakers' as they became known because of their quaking or shaking during their religious services. It was a defining moment for Fox as his ejection from the Minster signified his rejection by the Anglican Church. By the time he left York several people 'had received the truth' and a small meeting was established in the city in the years thereafter. Various preachers, including Fox, were imprisoned for their views, and in Fox's case at least, he spoke eloquently to the soldiers who arrested him. Fox was very successful in spreading his message and by the time of his death in 1691 there were nearly 50,000 'Friends'. Many of them emigrated to North America and it was there that the Quaker William Penn founded Pennsylvania in 1682, with its capital Philadelphia.

In the religious life of England the year 1662 is an important one. In that year the Act of Uniformity was passed which required all church ministers to agree with every word of the service of the Church of

England. Those that did not were labelled 'non-conformists', which included the Quaker and Baptist movements. Nationally between one and two thousand church ministers were forced out of their posts. In general the clergy of York favoured the Church of England and the Act caused little dissension within the city. Nationally there were pockets of short-lived resistance and one plot resulted in eighteen people being incarcerated in York Castle and executed at Tyburn in 1664. Their heads decorated the gateways of the city as a gruesome reminder of the fate of people who rebelled.

York Politics at the End of the Seventeenth Century

Following Charles II's death in 1685 his brother was crowned as King James II (1685–88). At first James was a popular king as in his last years King Charles had milked Royalist feeling and crushed any opposition. Yet James only lasted three years as king before being compelled to flee. The reason for his increasing unpopularity was his own religion.

James had a strong and passionate Catholic belief which he actively promoted despite ruling a largely Protestant country. James attempted to get Parliament to repel the Test Acts which barred Catholics from holding office. When this measure failed he required civic officials to answer three questions to state their position on the Test Acts. James's own view was made abundantly clear by his joyful reception of a papal nuncio – the Pope's representative – to his court. Other measures by James included packing civic government, the judiciary and armed forces with his own supporters, who were often Catholic.

Opposition to James's religious policies was led by members of the Minster who refused to accept them. The corporation took a more cautionary stance by offering very evasive answers to crown officials. The council played a dual game of at times supporting James whilst also supporting opposition to the king. They organised civic celebrations when James II's son was born, but also did not quell the rejoicing when seven bishops were acquitted for 'seditious libel'. The corporation's act was effectively an act of defiance against James. On the day of the acquittal of the seven bishops, the bishop of London and six important laymen invited James's Protestant daughter, Mary, and her husband William of Orange, to overthrow James.

William landed in Devon on 5 November 1688 and rather than stating that he wanted to be king, proclaimed that he was merely defending the rights of Protestants. As he marched towards London his own forces grew and James's army melted away. Mary and William became joint monarchs.

Whilst the transition from a Catholic king to Protestant king and queen was largely peaceful, in many places – including York – religious sentiment was running high. In the last months of 1688 there was a fear that the Catholics in the city would rise in support of James II. This lead to rioting by a Protestant mob in St Saviourgate, the seizure of the city gates by the city militia and the destruction of a Catholic chapel. Furthermore the militia ransacked the houses of suspected or known Catholics in York. Pictures and images were torn down, books and vestments seized and then in the evening they were burned on bonfires in Coney Street. Some Catholics were taken prisoner and whilst none were killed, a few had their estates seized.

At the end of the century York settled into the role of a busy, industrious market town and social centre. During the Civil War it had briefly become nationally important, but for the rest of the century its activities were of regional, rather than national importance.

CHAPTER SIX

Restoration and Georgian York, 1689–1837

The period between 1689 and 1837 was one of tremendous change due to the beginnings of the industrial revolution. These changes were felt particularly in the West Riding of Yorkshire in the industrial cities such as Bradford and Leeds. York however remained a society in which elegance and old money still paraded its wealth. The industrialisation of the city was for a later age.

York in the Late Seventeenth Century

York in the late seventeenth century was a bustling, energetic and largely confident city. Coffee houses and inns were places for merchants and lawyers to meet. The first coffee houses were established in York by 1669 and there were many in York by the end of the century. Swimming in the River Ouse was also a popular pastime, though not a particularly healthy one as people threw their rubbish into the river. Boating was also a favourite up and down the river. There was also bowling on the bowling greens and a more sedate, if potentially expensive, pastime was gambling and the playing of cards.

As well as a social centre, York was also at times a garrison city and troops were a constant, if irregular, feature of life in the city. In 1689 the Glorious Revolution – which resulted in William of Orange and Mary Stuart being crowned – had caused political upheaval in the country. York was no exception and in that year 5,000 foot soldiers and 1,000 horse wintered in York before journeying to Ireland to fight there.

The population of the city was overwhelmingly English, though there were a few immigrants, notably French Protestants called Huguenots who had fled severe persecution by the Catholic authorities in France.

In the 1660s York only had about 12,000 inhabitants, tiny by comparison with London's 575,000, but London was the largest capital in Europe. Other provincial cities were larger than York – Norwich with 30,000 and Bristol with 20,000, but the size of these cities was exceptional. Although York was at the bottom of the first division in terms of size of cities it was still an important regional capital.

LAW AND ORDER

During the eighteenth century crimes in the city ranged from the scandalous to the mundane, though the penalties could often be unreasonably vicious and harsh. As York had one of the important courts in Yorkshire, notorious criminals were sent to the castle to await punishment. Particularly severe punishment was meted out to wives who were convicted of poisoning their husbands. In 1767 Ann Sowerby of Whitby was put to death by hanging at the Tyburn gallows, the site of which was on the Tadcaster Road near the present day racecourse. After her death her body was burnt as additional punishment. The last instance of this happening occurred ten years later to Eliza Bordington, also at York, and these were the last such examples of women's bodies being burnt in Yorkshire.

Even relatively mild crimes could result in the death penalty and Thomas England was hanged for horse stealing in 1779, as was Dick Turpin whose story is told below. However, a large number of lesser infringements only resulted in a fine and it was the job of the city's constables to bring to court people who deposited piles of dirt and manure in the streets or allowed pigs to roam free through York. Other duties of the constables included arresting vagrants and those who refused to work. However, there was one basic problem with the system, which grew increasingly obvious as the population expanded: constables were only on duty during daylight hours.

When taken seriously, the role of constable was a tremendous drain on an individual's time and money. It is not surprising that many paid a deputy £10 to do the job for him. Helping, or perhaps at times hindering, the constables in their duties was a man paid by the city's corporation who had the unusual title of 'common informer'. He was the city's thief taker and the constables were expected to aid him in his work. However, the common informer could also hire himself out to investigate crimes.

In 1705 York County Gaol was completed. The design was revolutionary because for the first time in England, and maybe the world, architecture was used as 'an instigator of virtue' within a prison. The façade was a grand one and is more akin to a gentleman's country house or mansion than a normal prison of the times. Within, as without, there was a social and criminal hierarchy. At the bottom were the felons – small time thieves and crooks – and they were held in vaulted cellars. Debtors were in the upper echelons of the prison hierarchy and were often previously wealthy gentry or merchants who had fallen on hard times. Their families might pay for privileges such as better accommodation or food, and they were allowed to walk amongst the deer kept on the castle green and people of society who could also stroll there. Later, in 1777, a description of the internal conditions was written which contained a 'noble area of Debtors'. However, the cells for felons were seven and a half feet by six feet wide, 'close and dark', which housed three prisoners at night – in winter often for fourteen to sixteen hours a day – with only straw on the floor. Women felons were housed in another part of the prison, a feature which was a first in prison design.

The Jacobite Rebellion 1715

In 1715 the first of the two Jacobite rebellions occurred. The Jacobites supported James Stuart – son of the vanquished king, James II, who had fled England in 1688. James Stuart bided his time in France but in 1715 a series of three uprisings were planned in England and Scotland. The English government crushed two, but it was in Scotland that James received most support. His army of supporters marched south down the west side of the England, briefly capturing Preston in September 1715. James landed in Scotland a few months later in December, but without the promised aid of the French. During his six week stay he did little to help his own cause and support drifted away.

Despite all the action being on the west side of the country there was a degree of consternation in York, though this was quieted as the Jacobites retreated. The castle became the prison of a number of prominent rebels, though some escaped.

Defoe's View of York, 1720s

In the 1720s the novelist Daniel Defoe passed through York and recorded his impressions:

> York is indeed a pleasant and beautiful city . . . there is an abundance of good company here, and abundance of good families live here . . . No other city in England is better furnished with provisions of every kind, not any so cheap.

The Lord Mayor's Mansion House, 1726

Until 1724 the lord mayor of York had used his own house as a basis for his civic work, but at the end of every year all the mayoral paraphernalia, such as the staff of office, garments and other items had to be carried from the old lord mayor's house to the new one. Not surprisingly this was hardly satisfactory, though this system had lasted hundreds of years.

As the prestige of the city rested with the annually elected lord mayor of York, in 1724 the corporation decided that a new Mansion House was required to enhance the lord mayor's dignity. The result is the Mansion House that still stands today fronting St Helen's Square. Its exterior has an elegant simplicity about it, though inside its decoration was designed to impress visitors and dignitaries.

Even though not the first (that record belongs to Newcastle upon Tyne) the Mansion House in York was a pioneer in the field and the concept was soon copied by London on a larger scale. Despite the building's importance and extensive searches through the records the architect remains unknown.

The civic occasions were often colourful and theatrical and the city accounts regularly included the expenses for the lord mayor's day. Later in the century, in 1768, the parade expenses included carrying of the city colours, firemen, a drummer and the ringing of the bells of the Minster and in Coney Street.

Dick Turpin (1706–1739)

In his own lifetime Dick Turpin was one of a number of violent criminals and was not famous in his own right. His fame, through the writings of a Victorian novelist, would follow almost a century after his death.

Turpin was born in Essex and became part of a notorious group known as the Gregory Gang. The gang was ruthless and terrorised the villages and towns of Essex. Turpin became a member and after the gang was broken up he moved on to become a highwayman. Eventually his pursuers almost caught up with him and he journeyed north. He settled in Beverley as a gentleman, using the assumed name of John Palmer. To fund his lifestyle he often visited Lincolnshire to rustle cows and horses.

At first all went well and he lived comfortably, but gradually events conspired against him. A trivial incident whereby he killed his landlord's cockerel resulted in him appearing before the magistrates. They enquired into his lifestyle and gradually his exploits in Lincolnshire were discovered and he was arrested for horse theft.

His real identity as Dick Turpin the highwayman was still unknown, and on the horse theft charge he was imprisoned in York Castle. It was here that his true identity was revealed by an amazing coincidence. As he waited in his cell Turpin wrote to his brother for help. Unfortunately his brother refused to pay the sixpence for the letter and it was returned to the local post office. There Turpin's old schoolmaster, Mr Smith, recognised Turpin's handwriting and his true identity was revealed and he was sentenced to death.

Even at his hanging at Tyburn, Turpin still managed to be the centre of attention by creating an impressive funeral spectacle. He hired five professional mourners to follow him to the scaffold and he acted up for the crowd. On the scaffold-ladder he jumped off and hung himself, thereby grimly outwitting his captors.

However, the story of Dick Turpin does not end, even after death.

Turpin was buried, but a labourer called Richard Hogg dug up the body and carried it to the garden of one Marmaduke Palms. Palms was a surgeon who paid Hogg to exhume the body illegally for medical dissection. The practice was much feared throughout England and Scotland as it disturbed the resting place of the dead. Hogg the labourer can have been not as discreet as required because an angry mob soon gathered at Palms' house. The constables were called and Palms and Hogg were arrested and fined. Thereafter Turpin's body rested in peace.

Even so, Turpin would have been only a minor character in the history of York had it not been for an international bestseller written almost a hundred years after Turpin's death. In 1834 Harrison Ainsworth wrote a novel called *Rookwood* in which Turpin rode his horse Black Bess from Westminster to York. Ainsworth's description of the ride was fast-paced and exciting and thereafter Turpin and Black Bess became cemented in the public's imagination. Whilst the story is a good one, the real criminal who rode from the south to York was John 'Nick' Nevison. In 1676 he robbed a sailor in Kent. To give himself an alibi he rode 190 miles to York in just fifteen hours and calmly had a game of bowls with the lord mayor at 8 p.m. He soon became known as 'Swift Nicks'. His alibi worked, but further crimes resulted in him

The notorious Dick Turpin's gravestone

The supposed ride of Dick Turpin and Black Bess from Westminster to York as
fabricated by the 19th century author Harrison Ainsworth

being arrested and hanged in York in 1684, twenty-two years before
Turpin was born.

The Second Jacobite Rebellion 1745

The second Jacobite attempt by James Stuart to seize the throne of
England came in 1745. This time Bonnie Prince Charlie, son of James
Stuart and grandson of James II, led the Scottish forces and on this
occasion the rising of the clans and their progress was more successful.
The Prince landed on 23 July 1745 and despite an initial lack of men,
captured Falkirk and then Edinburgh. From Edinburgh the Jacobites
could have marched southwards either via Newcastle and then
Yorkshire, or through Lancashire.

The possibility of a Jacobite attack caused agitation in York and
military preparations began. Archbishop Herring preached a sermon in
the Minster against the rebels and this was followed by a public meeting
in the grounds of the castle aimed at recruiting volunteers. The
resultant military force was called the Yorkshire Association, which was
largely made up the nobility, clergy and gentry of Yorkshire. The fox

hunting gentry of the county formed the Royal Regiment of Hunters. This regiment went north and was involved in a skirmish with the retreating Jacobite forces near Penrith.

Preparations were also made to defend York. The corporation took action to survey and patch up the city walls and two regimental groups were formed: the Blues and Independents. Neither saw direct action and both were disbanded within the year, but they showed that York had the capacity to defend itself if the need arose.

The final decisive battle of the Jacobite rising took place on 16 April 1746 when the Jacobite army was decisively crushed at Culloden by the English forces led by the duke of Cumberland. By this time the threat had subsided, but the presence of the Jacobites in York was maintained, because two heads of executed rebels were placed in Micklegate Bar in 1745. They remained there for nine years until in 1754 a tailor in York, William Arundell, stole them with assistance from two Irish journeymen. Unfortunately the two Irishmen informed upon William and he was imprisoned for two years.

The Stately Homes of Yorkshire

Grand houses and castles had always been a feature of the Yorkshire landscape since the Middle Ages. The sale of the monastic buildings and lands resulted in the monasteries becoming private or crown property and being used either as quarries for stone, or the shells of new stately homes. In York the lodging house of the abbot of St Mary's Abbey became the King's Manor and in the countryside Newburgh Priory became a stately home. Following the closure of the abbey at Whitby, the abbey buildings were used to build a magnificent home for the Cholmley family.

However, it was in the late seventeenth and eighteenth centuries some of the very greatest examples of stately homes were built. Following the Civil War, Yorkshire's strategic importance declined, and as the country became more peaceful and prosperous the wealthy landowners created luxurious houses for themselves. Close to York there are the magnificent examples of Castle Howard, begun in 1701 and designed in flamboyant baroque style by Sir John Vanbrugh, Beningbrough Hall and Harewood House, which was partially designed by the York architect John Carr.

As well as the interiors, the stately homes were positioned in large and fabulous landscapes. The water gardens and landscape of Studley Royal, which contains the remains of Fountains Abbey, has been recognised as a World Heritage Site because of its international importance and history. Studley Royal has curving terrace walks through woodland with vistas across the lakes, with classical style temples beyond. The parkland of Castle Howard is on an altogether larger scale and stretches from the house into the distance across a lake. The gardens at Castle Howard are rather formal, whilst the parkland is less so and contains many classical style temples and a mausoleum situated on a hill and visible for miles around.

GEORGIAN ARCHITECTURE IN YORK

The grand architecture of York is dominated by Georgian architecture. The buildings are a combination of the grand and elaborate, such as the Mansion House or the ornate and spectacular Assembly Rooms, or the more common but elegant Georgian houses and shops.

Today Fairfax House on Castlegate is one of the finest Georgian house in the city, having been rescued and restored to its former glory by the York Civic Trust in 1984. Although it existed before, the house was completely remodelled by the York architect John Carr for Viscount Fairfax. Fairfax had married twice: his first wife died within a year and his second wife was a distant cousin, Mary Fairfax. Tragedy struck when his wife and all but one of his children died of smallpox and so he moved from London to York with Anne his one remaining child. The house was remodelled for Anne and it was the York town house for the family, with the family's major country seat being at Gilling Castle.

Fairfax House was lavishly furnished and decorated and reflected Fairfax's tastes. In the library are plaster medallions on the ceiling showing John Milton, Joseph Addison, John Locke and Alexander Pope, all of whose writings Fairfax admired.

The corporation was well aware of the possibilities that civic improvements offered and financed New Walk which is still today a pleasant walk beside the river from Fishergate towards Fulford lined with trees. Another tree planting scheme was that along the walls from Monk Bar to Gillygate along Lord Mayor's Walk. Building schemes within the city included the development of New Street between Davygate and Coney Street.

However, most of the changes came about by wealthy gentry or traders wanting to modernise their properties and make them more fashionable. For those who could afford it new Georgian frontages were placed onto the medieval structures which survived behind.

York's most famous architect was John Carr. From humble beginnings he quickly gained an excellent reputation and for the majority of his working life he lived in York becoming one of its wealthiest citizens. He formed a solid clientele in the city and many of his fine houses still survive, such as houses on Bootham and Micklegate and the previously mentioned Fairfax House which is open to the public. By 1766 Carr's reputation, wealth and status were demonstrated by his own new house on Skeldergate (number 18) which he designed and built and can still be seen today.

DIRT AND DISEASE

Amidst all the Georgian splendour there were continuing worries about the levels of pollution. There was the perennial concern that animals being brought into the city would be slaughtered in unlicensed locations. The potential for this was so great that in 1768 the corporation drew up a proforma wording for punishing would-be offenders which stated that a the setting up of a 'slaughterhouse and dunghill or soil hole for the killing and slaying of beasts' would lead to 'divers noisome, filthy and unwholesome smells from the excrement, blood, entrails, offals and other filth' for which there would be a maximum penalty. The corporation also took a few steps towards cleaning the city and a man was paid 19 shillings and 6 pence for sweeping outside Monk Bar.

John Goodricke

Although York was comparatively minor in importance in scientific and artistic endeavour compared to the larger cities, especially London, there were several notable personalities who lived for a time in York.

In the scientific field one of the most notable was the astronomer John Goodricke, (1764–1786). He was born in Germany, the son of a British diplomat and became deaf at an early age, possibly because of scarlet fever. However, his parents sent him first to a progressive school in Edinburgh and then to Warrington Academy. Warrington Academy was a centre of intellectual thought and had such tutors as Joseph Priestly, Jean Paul Marat, and William Enfield. Goodricke excelled in mathematics and after finishing his schooling returned home to his parents, who were now living in York. He was fortunate in making friends with Edward Pigott, whose father had one of only three private astronomical observatories in England at that time. John and Edward began observing the heavens and John soon became fascinated by the way certain stars altered their brightness over a few days. Night after night John studied the stars and his keen observational technique became the standard test for determining a star's variable brightness.

At the age of only nineteen he presented his first paper to the prestigious Royal Society in London and in the following year he was presented with the Godfrey Copley Medal for the most significant discovery in science. Two years later, at the age of twenty-one, he was elected a Fellow of the Royal Society. Two weeks later he was dead from pneumonia, probably caused by his long exposure to the chill and damp night air. In recognition of his achievements one of the colleges at the university is called Goodricke College in his honour.

LITERATURE

The two best known people in the literary world connected with York were the author Laurence Sterne and Daniel Defoe's character Robinson Crusoe. Robinson Crusoe was described by Defoe as 'of York, mariner' who was 'born in 1632, in the city of York, of a good family, though not of that country'. The reference to Crusoe being a mariner showed that sea and river trade were still an important part of York's economy, though it was an industry in terminal decline. Although a fictional character Defoe based Crusoe on the real life Alexander Selkirk who stayed alone on a Pacific island between 1704 and 1709.

The most famous Georgian author connected with York is Laurence

Sterne (1713-1768). He was born in Ireland, went to Cambridge University and afterwards obtained a living as a clergyman just outside York at Sutton on the Forest. During his life he also was in charge of Stillington and Coxwold churches, and became a prebendary at York Minster. Sterne's greatest work is *Tristram Shandy,* first published in 1760, and in its rambling account it reflects the author's humorous and whimsical opinions on life. The carefully crafted shapeless muddle of a novel was a new invention – before writers had sought a careful shape and structure to their novels.

Given Sterne's York connections with the Minster and parishes it is not surprising that some York characters feature in Sterne's writings. The most famous characterisation was that of Dr John Burton who became 'Dr Slop' in *Tristram Shandy.* An element of Sterne's dislike for Burton was their diametrical political and religious views.

THEATRE

The origins of the theatrical performance in York stretch back to the early thirteenth century and reached their height during the Medieval Mystery Plays, but by the eighteenth century the main focus for theatrical performance was the Theatre Royal. The origins of the theatre date from 1744 when the cloisters of the former St Leonard's Hospital were leased as a theatre. The person who dominated the theatre's history in the eighteenth century was Tate Wilkinson (1739–1803). He was originally an actor on the London stage and knew well such actors as Garrick, which in turn led him into the same social circle as Doctor Johnson and other literary giants. Tate had acted in York twice before he became 'Master of the Theatre Royal' in 1770. The theatre was in a dilapidated state as the former owner, Mr Baker, had run out of money and had applied to Tate for a loan, which was duly forthcoming and had meant that Tate was Baker's natural successor. As well as York, Tate also managed other satellite theatres on the northern circuit in Hull, Wakefield, Leeds, Pontefract, Doncaster and Beverley, with the further opportunity of using Sheffield as well

The playgoers in a Georgian theatre ranged from the very rich to the poor and the audience was not the quiet, attentive (or if not attentive, silently asleep) one which is known today. A Georgian audience was noisy, boisterous and not averse to calling out requests or making their views known by hurling things at the actors. Tate had to subdue several riots and in 1791 the audience even attempted to set fire to the theatre. These and many other instances of theatre life are contained in Tate's memoirs.

DRINK

Alcoholic drink was an integral part of life in York and in 1577 it was estimated that York, with a population *c.* 20,000 had a third of all the inns in the whole of Yorkshire.

Many of the inns would have been small, with their own beer or ale brewing capabilities, and households too brewed ale or beer. Higher up the scale were the moderately large inns and taverns which may have bought in beer, and at the top of the social scale were the inns for higher levels of society which sold wines and spirits. The supplying of these establishments was a regional affair, with suppliers either importing the spirits directly through Hull or setting up warehouses in Leeds or York.

With this amount of alcohol and no restrictions on age or opening hours, it is not surprising that drunkenness was often of concern for the authorities. During the eighteenth century there were, however, an increasing number of alternatives to alcohol. Water from wells – or from the River Ouse – and milk had always been an option. In the case of milk, people rich enough either kept their own cows or could buy milk from the milkmaids who travelled daily to the city from the nearby farms.

The new options available were coffee, tea and hot chocolate, all at first extravagant luxuries which came down in price as their popularity rose and the quantities imported increased. The new social dimension was the rise of the coffee shops. These started in London and quickly became popular in the provinces. York was no exception and several are known – the most famous being called Parker's which was frequented by the gentry and merchant classes.

CANALS, ROADS AND SEDAN CHAIRS

The eighteenth and early nineteenth centuries witnessed many innovations in transportation of people and goods. In the early nineteenth century the railways grew in importance, but in the latter part of the previous century the two innovations were canals and toll roads. The location of York on two navigable rivers, the Ouse and the Foss, meant that transportation by purpose built canals was less important than other places which had no rivers or problems with navigation. However, to improve access a dam was built at Naburn Lock which raised the level of the water (which previously could be as shallow as ten inches at low tide) and parts of the Foss were canalised to improve the sluggish flow of that river. The money for these ventures came from tolls charged on commodities using the rivers. The general charge was six pence a ton, but the price for wine rose to two shillings and six pence a ton.

Some roads too underwent a great improvement by the adoption of the toll or turnpike system. The toll roads were well maintained and fast, but in return a charge was made for vehicles using them. In total there were 153 miles of toll roads leading into York from the sur-rounding areas, the busiest of which was the section of road between Tadcaster and York. The toll roads were controlled by the toll gate keepers who took the money for travelling on the road, but they could also report coachmen for reckless driving and checked the height of luggage on coaches. As the system evolved, weighing machines were installed to make sure that carts or coaches were not overladen as heavy carts could damage roads. The level of payment was based on the assumption of wear upon the road that would occur. The charges for the Tadcaster to York turnpike included one shilling (twelve pence) for a coach and six horses, eight pence for a coach and four horses, two pence for a coach and two horses and one pence for a horse and rider. Flocks of sheep, lambs or pigs were charged at five pence for every twelve animals.

Within cities and towns a new form of personal travel in the eighteenth century was the sedan chair. A sedan chair was a box like structures with long handles, which enabled two men to carry the hirer inside. The advantages included not tripping in the street and avoiding the mud and dirt of the York pavements. The first known sedan chairs in England were used in London in the second decade of the 1600s and they spread in popularity through the country. There were two sorts: personal, where a rich person would have their own chair and chair-men to carry them, and chairs for public hire. The public hire chairs were certainly established in York by 1724 and the fare paid was determined by the distance travelled. A short ride of under half a mile cost six pence. Fares were markedly increased if called out after 10 p.m. at night. The London chairman had the reputation of being tough Irishmen. In York the carriers were more civil, though not averse to the odd practical joke, such as causing the occupant to fall out, or loosen the bottom so the hirer had to trot along too. Whilst never very numerous, sedan chairs were a familiar sight in York with twenty or so public hire chairs during the eighteenth century. Sedan chairs continued well into the nineteenth century and even as late as 1857 there were two chairs in York.

YORK RACECOURSE

Horsing racing in York was originally located just outside the city at Clifton Ings and there were races being held there by 1709, but in 1731 the site of the race course was moved to its current location at the Knavesmire. The marquis of Rockingham was particularly keen on horse racing and commissioned John Carr to erect the first grandstand. To this day there is a race run every October with the Rockingham name.

A visiting racegoer, Simon Scrope, wrote in 1731

> Tomorrow we set out for York to see the new horse course, lately made on Knavesmire, and to join in the great goings of the week, the life of which no town or city can compare with for gaiety, sport and company all of one mind.

A ROYAL VISIT AND FEAST 1789

Royal visitors to York were not uncommon and they were dined and wined by the mayor and corporation. In 1789 the future prince regent – eldest son of George III – made a visit to York which was greeted with immense enthusiasm by the people. He graciously attended the races (to gamble) and rode through the cheering crowds on horseback. Afterwards the citizens were so exuberant that they uncoupled the horses from his carriage and pulled it into town.

A few days later he attended a feast given by the city which included three 'Pine-Apples' and three turtles, one of which had been trans-ported to York with an armed guard.

THE FOUNDATION OF THE RETREAT, 1796

The Retreat, located between the city and Heslington, was an asylum founded by William Tuke. Its revolutionary principles were based on Tuke's own Quaker ethos that an inner 'Light' of 'substance, reality, unity and peace' is within everyone. This was contrasted with the dark, which indicated 'shadow, deceit, multiplicity and strife'. That the 'Light' was peaceful and non-violent was an important aspect in relation to the treatment of the insane. Until the foundation of The Retreat, it was the standard practice to chain or lock up the insane and when necessary to use violence or force to restrain them. Furthermore the insane were often figures of fun and amusement and the most famous hospital, at Bethlem in London (popularly known as Bedlam) was regularly visited by the social élite to pity or laugh at the inmates.

The Retreat, however, was based on very different principles whereby minimum force or restraint was used, there were no bars on the windows, the buildings were airy and light, and there were large well planted grounds for the residents to walk in. Staff and patients were known collectively as 'The Family'. The internal organisation of the Retreat was written about by Samuel Tuke (William's grandson) in 1813. Although The Retreat was principally for Quakers, it accepted anyone, though there were different charges: eight shillings a week for the poorest non-Quakers and four shillings for the poorest Quakers. There was also a hierarchy of provision within The Retreat which reflected the outside world: the more money a patient or family had, the better the accommodation. For the richest patients, personal ser-vants were allowed.

The Retreat was groundbreaking in many ways, not only in the treatment of its patients, but also in setting up a half-way house (known as 'The Appendage') 'for those needing least supervision'. Amongst the staff, women were key to the efficient running of The Retreat and, probably in theory rather than practice, had equal influence as the men.

The new practices at The Retreat had a great influence not only in Britain but across the world. Samuel Tuke's description of 1813, which sold over a thousand copies, led to more humane asylums in America and Europe. Two years later a Parliamentary Committee was set to monitor asylums more closely because of the public response to Tuke's work. The Retreat at York was a new model for asylums and led the world in its treatment of its patients.

THE MILITARY AND THE CREATION OF THE YORK GARRISON, 1796

Until the last decade of the eighteenth century there was no permanent military presence in York, though troops had often been billeted in the inns or houses around the city. The presence of the military was a double-edged sword for the citizens. In 1777, the feared naval 'press gang' were in York searching for able-bodied men who were bribed, or simply abducted, into the navy. Fortunately the press gang was a rarity in the city, rather it was the army who were increasingly part of city life as the century progressed. In the late eighteenth century a noted military hero was Major Peirson who, in 1779, recruited the 95th Regiment in York. The Regiment was sent to Jersey to help defend the Channel Islands against French attack. The French landed in 1781 and controlled St Helier's town square. Pierson led his troops against them and was killed before the main attack, but his troops rallied and defeated the French. He was considered a notable hero in York at the time and a painting survives at the Tate Gallery of his death.

In the 1790s there was considerable military concern, especially with the rise of Napoleon to power in France. In 1794 a body of infantry was raised in York, with the corporation giving £500 towards its costs. In 1796 the first permanent cavalry barracks were built in the city at Fulford. The barracks were part of a much larger campaign by the then prime minister, William Pitt the Younger, to prepare the country for war against the French and barracks were built in many cities across the country.

The arrangements within the barracks were primitive. It was the custom for a married soldier to acquire a corner of the barrack hut, not only for himself but also for his wife and children. A margin of privacy was maintained by hanging blankets to form a curtain. This arrangement was so common that it was recognised by the military authorities and rules and regulations were drawn up. The number of wives permitted was limited to one per room of twelve soldiers. The duties of a 'permitted wife' were also regulated and she was required to cook, clean, sew and launder. The presence of a wife was also seen as a curb to the soldier's drunkenness.

COMMERCE, TRADE AND AGRICULTURE

By the late eighteenth century York had become a social centre for the rich. The grand buildings added to the city's elegance, the new race course was a major attraction and the theatre had improved the city's culture. But elsewhere in Yorkshire changes were transforming the industrial practices of England. New inventions, such as the steam engine and powered looms meant that the production of cloth – for centuries the preserve of craftsmen working in their own homes – now became concentrated in ever larger factories. The towns of the West Riding of Yorkshire became a focus of the Industrial Revolution.

Behind York's genteel veneer, the people of the city were making their livings through trade. There was no one dominant industry, rather there were a host of minor, and sometimes surprising, trades. Within the city there were textile workers using linen, wool, cotton as well as weavers of lace and silk. There were three silk weavers in York in the 1780s. There were several metal working firms, and York had a long tradition of bell founding – stretching back to the Middle Ages – which continued into the eighteenth century. More mundane products were also made such as lamps, garden utensils and small objects such as pastry cutters.

In any Georgian city the production of clothing, and selling of food and drink, were the basic staples of a city's trade. York was no exception. There were tanneries in Walmgate to make leather for clothing, three glove and four stocking manufactures and many boot and shoe makers. Brewing was a common occupation with sixteen common brewhouses in York in 1784. Alternative and more luxurious drinks could be bought and the Quaker family firm of Tuke's sold tea, coffee and chocolate. Corn was also ground in the city, either at the

City Mills, or at any one of a large number of windmills scattered across York's hinterland. These have all but disappeared, though a later windmill survives in Windmill Rise off Holgate Road, and the base of a windmill can be seen on the A64 past Tadcaster.

York was also the place of two more unusual industries. The first was ship building especially from the 1760s until the end of the century and three 100-ton brigandines were built, though this was the largest size possible as Naburn Lock downstream limited ship sizes. The second manufacture was that of combs. York was the centre of a considerable comb industry and the combs were made of horn, tortoiseshell or ivory. York combs are known to have been sold as far afield as London and Liverpool.

Whilst there was no one dominant industry during the middle of the eighteenth century York did have a claim to fame as the largest collecting point in the country for wholesale butter to be shipped to London. The butter came from the farms of the Vale of York and the strict checking of the quality of butter through York meant that it was much in demand in London. It is estimated that in the Vale 30,000 cows were kept to make butter. The wholesale trade of butter was conducted through a building called the Butter Stand or Standard which stood in the graveyard of St Martin-cum-Gregory in Micklegate, and Micklegate itself was the centre of the trade. Butter was stored in cellars and warehouses along the street. The volume of the butter trade was considerable and in 1769 80,000 firkins (a firkin is equivalent to nine gallons) of butter passed through York. Thereafter the trade declined as competition from overseas and London's hinterland resulted in less demand for Yorkshire butter.

Whereas the Industrial Revolution of the eighteenth century did not directly affect York, the agricultural changes had some indirect effect. A common practice was for the enclosure of fields, whereby one landlord came to own land previously owned by many families. Through these practices many people were driven from the land and sought work in York. However, the other consequences of these changes, and improved farming practices, resulted in higher yields and more crops, which increased the amount of produce being sold in York's markets.

FISHING DAY, 1819

Fishing day was an ancient ceremony performed by the mayor and corporation once every seven years to protect the rights of the city to its fishery between York and the mouth of the River Wharf downstream. By the later Georgian period it had turned into a major occasion at which little expense was spared. The expenses of fishing day in 1768 included over eleven stone of beef, three large hams, twenty-four fowl, veal lobsters and crabs. But it is the amount of drink that is astonishing: three gallons of brandy, four dozen barrels of red port, two dozen of white wine, twenty gallons of ale, five gallons of beer and six quarts of porter. It was obviously thirsty work being rowed downstream. One of the last entries shows the consequences of so much alcohol: 'glasses and plates broke, seven shillings and six pence'.

The details of the fishing day are given in greater detail in 1819. Nets were thrown into the River Ouse at the ancient and accustomed places. The party then returned to Naburn where according to custom they enjoyed an excellent dinner and returned to the city after dark at about 11 o'clock. In 1819 the catch had included a fine salmon of twenty lbs which was caught near Acaster, but in historical terms this was a poor catch: in 1631 forty-one salmon and other fish had been caught.

IMPROVEMENTS

In the eighteenth and nineteenth centuries there was a desire to open up the narrow streets of the city. In 1819 the corporation minutes recorded that the south and east walls of one of York's historic churches, St Michael's Spurriergate, should be reduced in length by six feet, a task which would be 'very desirable and of great public utility'. This was a relatively small project – a much larger one undertaken by the council was the creation of St Leonard's Place in 1834. This is one of the grandest and most magnificent nineteenth century terraces in York, which swept away the previous relatively poor buildings to create a wide street for carriages and 'genteel private residences'.

Improvements however were not always welcome and when the historic fabric of the city was at stake – especially the city walls – there was fierce controversy. The walls were often portrayed as an expensive nuisance owing to their high maintenance cost and serving no real use. The last time they could have been of use was during the Jacobite Rebellion of 1745, but in the end the Scots came nowhere near York. The walls also put a boundary around the heart of the city making new roads and houses difficult to plan for. However, despite these arguments there were vociferous campaigns to protect the walls and the other medieval buildings. This was augmented by national politics, for whilst across the Channel Napoleon was bringing in new architectural styles in the first part of the nineteenth century, in England the medieval gothic buildings of such places as York were seen as patriotic.

A passionate advocate of the character of York and keeping the walls was William Etty, but many others, locally and nationally, also argued for them. Many sections of wall were repaired, at considerable cost, but there were some losses, notably the barbicans of Bootham Bar and Micklegate Bar. However the corporation did repair the unfashionable areas of the walls around Walmgate.

In the early nineteenth century there was also an awakening of commercial activity within the city with its growing population and four new banks opened between 1810 and 1830 and a gasworks in 1823. The markets were also prosperous and the cattle market was moved outside the walls at Walmgate in 1826 with pens for 616 cattle and 6750 sheep being built. Four years later an extra four thousand pens were added.

JONATHAN MARTIN BURNS THE MINSTER, 1829

On the afternoon of 1 February 1829 Jonathan Martin concealed himself behind a monument in the Minster and waited until nightfall. When the church was dark and silent he crept out of his hiding place. He first of all prepared his escape route and then returned to the choir, piled cushions and prayer books into a large heap and set fire to them. Once they were burning to his satisfaction he made his escape and vanished into the night

In the early hours the fire was spotted and the primitive fire engines were called to the raging inferno. Molten lead from the roof dripped down and the fire was so intense that the limestone pillars were cracking under the heat

By the afternoon the fire was beginning to die out but the devas-

The non-conformist, Jonathan Martin who burnt the Minster in 1829

tation was enormous. Approximately 230 feet of the roof of the choir had come crashing down, and the fire had destroyed the medieval choir stalls, the organ, the pulpit.

The reason for Martin's actions was his blind hatred of formal prayers and order of service that was used by the Church of England. Rather Martin believed that all prayer should come directly from the heart, a belief followed by many non-conformist sects of the time. Martin's views led him to publish pamphlets against the clergy, including one in which called the clergy 'saarpents and vipears of Hell ... who Eyes stand out with fatness and still criing out mor Plum Pudding and Rost Beffe' (as he himself noted, his spelling and grammar were not strong points).

Martin's background was eventful. He was born near Hexham in Northumberland and was first apprenticed as tanner but on a trip to London was press-ganged into the navy. He began to rise through the ranks but during a naval action he fell into the freezing Baltic sea. He was only rescued after twenty minutes in the icy-cold water. It was after this that some people detected a change in his character.

After his release from the navy, he sold pamphlets detailing his life story up to that point. Amazingly he was reasonably successful and he printed a third edition which ran to a very respectable five thousand copies. His religious fervour against Church of England clergy began to take over his life and his first violent action was preparing to shoot the bishop of Oxford. Martin was put into an asylum, from which he escaped, and once again mingled with society. By many accounts he was a normal, peaceable citizen, who was married with children. The fact that marked him out was his intense loathing of the clergy of York Minster. It was this hatred which led him to burn the Minster.

After the fire he left the city but otherwise did little to hide and was soon caught. His trial was a great public spectacle and he loved the attention. It was fashionable for the ladies and gentlemen of the highest levels of society to sit in the galleries and watch the trial. The trial hinged on Martin's sanity. Various expert witnesses diagnosed his state of mind and a surgeon at the Retreat outside York described him as a 'monomaniac', that is he was normal except for his one theme of insanity. The jury found him 'not guilty' because of his insanity and he ended his days in a London hospital where he died in May 1838.

CHAPTER SEVEN

Victorian York,
1837–1901

Queen Victoria ruled between 1837–1901 and the years of her reign saw the change of England from a predominantly rural economy to an industrial one. During the course of her sixty-three year reign the British Empire was greatly expanded into Africa, and included India, Australia and Canada. It was an Empire on which the sun never set.

In the late 1830s and 1840s York was not an industrial town and it had been overtaken in population, size and prosperity by the industrial towns of the West Riding: Leeds, Bradford, Sheffield to name but three. Even so, York was a major regional centre serving the agricultural areas of the Vale of York and remained a key market place. Furthermore it was a magnet for the poor looking for work. Between 1801 and 1841 the population more than doubled from 2,479 houses to 5,958 houses and this rapid growth in population and the infrastructure of the city led to increasing concerns about the possibility of disease, a concern which became all too true in 1832.

Health and the Cholera Epidemic, 1832

The public health of York was always of concern to the city's authorities, particularly so when there was an outbreak of serious diseases. For centuries plague and disease had been a feature of life in York and England, but the combination of the massive expansion of the population, the growth in terrible slum areas and the inadequate sewage systems was a recipe for disaster.

There were two ways of disposing of sewage (called 'night soil'). The first was to dig a hole in the back yard (a 'privy') which was used by one or more households. In an extreme case five privies in the slum area of Bedern were used by three hundred people. The second method was to pile up sewage, which was then collected by 'night soil men'. Larger piles were made in the street and then transported to larger still piles at Layerthorpe Bridge and near St Margaret's Church, Walmgate. The health problems with this system are self evident and the smell must have been appalling, but more seriously there was a serious danger of effluent seeping into houses and into the water supply.

The water supply in Victorian York was a constant problem, especially for the rapidly growing numbers of the poor. The wealthier had more options and some, such as the Rowntree family, filtered the water supplied to them, or had their own deep wells, but even these could become contaminated. Those who could afford it were supplied by the York Waterworks Company which pumped water to houses or taps in the yard, though the water that was pumped came straight from the River Ouse. The poorer areas had communal wells which were often little more than shallow holes. An alternative was to take water from the Rivers Ouse and Foss, but they were also the dumping grounds for rubbish and so were heavily polluted.

It is no wonder in these conditions that disease was rife, especially in the poorer districts. Some courtyards and streets had a particularly bad reputation. One of the worst was formally called Beedham's Court, but its widespread nickname was 'Hagworm's Nest'. This courtyard was located across the river in Skeldergate and was the starting place for many outbreaks of disease. Other desperately unhygienic areas were in the slums of Bedern near the Minster and in the Walmgate area, a popular area for the destitute immigrants to settle.

The disease which caused the greatest fear and hysteria was cholera, though ironically it was not the greatest killer. There were two major outbreaks, one in 1832 and the other in 1848. It was recorded that the first person to be afflicted was called Thomas Hughes, a 'poor man of intemperate habits'. The 1832 outbreak lasted from June until October and whilst it killed 185 people, 265 who also caught the disease recovered. To this day a lasting memorial stands to the victims of the epidemic – a small plot of land between the city walls and the railway station was used as cemetery and twenty gravestones can still be seen.

However, if you were wealthy enough there were very pleasant parts of York to live in such as Micklegate, with its fine Georgian houses, and also outside the city walls in such areas as The Mount and in Clifton. In the areas outside the city walls there were often tree lined roads and a much lower density of housing and people, creating a middle class haven with more sanitary conditions and consequently lower levels of disease.

YORK PUBLIC CEMETERY OPENED IN 1836

Adding to the general level of disease was the state of the city's graveyards. Until the middle of the nineteenth century the only places available for burial were the graveyards attached to the medieval churches of the city. With a rapidly expanding population and a high death rate the problem of burial became acute with layers upon layers of burials inside and outside churches, most of which were in the heart of the city. One consequence of burials in church was that the floor level rose. In St Helen's Stonegate the situation before it was rebuilt became so bad that there was a danger of hitting one's head on the roof supports.

The solution was to build a civic cemetery away from the city centre, which was achieved in 1836. The land was divided into two, each with its own chapel, one for burials under the rites of the Church of England, and the other for the Dissenting Churches.

There were strict guidelines and prices for burial in the cemetery and a single burial cost ten shillings and sixpence. A horse and carriage could be hired to carry the body and six mourners for six shillings. There was a concern that the poorest members of society should also receive burial and so for occupants of houses rated under £5 the fees were halved. The most expensive place to be buried was under one of the chapels, and eight such burials (presumably for a family) cost £30.

There was also concern that the graves should not be disturbed, for there was still a fear that bodies might be removed for scientific experiments. Therefore there was a strict regulation that 'no human remains should be dug up or disturbed' and there was provision for guarding the cemetery at night.

The Irish Potato Famine

Like many cities in England, and across the world, York was directly affected by the Irish Potato Famine victims who fled Ireland to escape the starvation in their homeland. The poverty stricken Irish had to settle in the cheapest, and most run down, communities in the city and so the greatest concentrations were in the Walmgate area, Bedern and Minster Yard. The direct railway links across the Pennines between the port of Liverpool and York further increased the number of Irish immigrants.

The poverty of the Irish, along with their different customs, religion and sometimes violent ways, proved to be a problem for the authorities as they struggled to keep order and a disease free city.

The Chartist Movement in York

The Chartist Movement was a campaign to introduce reforms into the English political system. The Movement was predominantly a mass working-class organisation which flourished in times of hunger and desperation, especially in rapidly expanding northern industrial cities. By 1838 there were over one hundred Chartist organisations around the country which sought to improve the lot of the working class by making elections and politics fairer.

The Chartist Movement was based on a six point charter which demanded secret ballots, universal male suffrage, equal electoral districts, payment for Members of Parliament (MPs), that MPs did not have to own property, and annual elections.

In the late 1830s and 1840s York was not an industrial town to the same extent as Leeds or the other great metropolitan cities of the north and for several years had only a small Chartist following. A major, if temporary, boost to the Chartist cause in York was the presence of a radical Chartist, Feargus O'Connor, when he was imprisoned in York Castle. Even though imprisoned O'Connor was wealthy and influential enough to have a comfortable lifestyle. Before being put in prison he was shown the sights of York, and whilst in prison he was allowed to furnish his room according to his own taste and his meals were cooked by one of the inns of the city. O'Connor's release led to one of the great political demonstrations of Victorian York on the Knavesmire, which included Chartist contingents from Nottingham, Scarborough, Selby and Malton. O'Connor himself arrived dressed in a suit of black velvet in a carriage pulled by six black horses.

For the next three years Chartism in York was a powerful political force and in 1842 O'Connor – now the leader of the Chartist movement – once again spoke in York. Politically the Chartists supported the local Tory politicians and it was probably with the Tories encouragement that the Chartists prospered. The Chartist movement appealed to those skilled and semi-skilled workers such as shoemakers, tailors and stonemasons. In 1842 the York Chartists instituted a series of fund raising initiatives such as social functions and balls, and supporters had the chance to buy Crow and Tyrel's Chartist Breakfast Powder at the Chartist headquarters in Fossgate. Such events were in contrast to the more military and violent solutions advocated by Chartists from the more industrial towns who were imprisoned in York gaol.

During the middle years of the 1840s the slowly improving economic situation lessened the passion behind the Chartist Movement until 1848 when a severe depression once again caused a brief upsurge in membership. Once again militant Chartists from industrial cities were imprisoned in York Castle whilst more moderate York chartists awaited a massive national revival, which failed to materialise and thereafter both the national movement and the branch in York declined and faded away.

LIFE IN 1851

Records from the year 1851 give an excellent snap shot of life in York in the nineteenth century as the industrial revolution began to make changes in the city. Two important censuses took place in that year – the first was the national census which recorded the names, addresses, ages, occupations of every person in the country. A similar census had taken place in 1841, but the 1851 census included the information about where a person was born, a detail which is invaluable for family historians. The second census in the same year was the religious census described below. The third event took place in London – the Great Exhibition in the Crystal Palace.

The 1851 national census gives a view of occupations in York. The industry of York in 1851 was broadly the same as it was one hundred years earlier and reflected a pre-industrial town with a high proportion of the population being employed as domestic servants looking after their wealthier masters and mistresses. Other occupations were small scale – shopkeepers or tailors, milliners, food providers and market gardeners.

Even though some great railway entrepreneurs were based in York – notably George Hudson, the Railway King – there were relatively few jobs in the railways at this point. The real growth happened in the second half of the century.

Elsewhere there were a few modest industrial concerns which were laying the roots for further industrial expansion. There were six iron foundries in York, all within the city walls. Most provincial foundries served local needs, and walking around York today and looking at drainage covers many of the names of the foundries can be seen, such as the foundry of William Dove. However, it was the iron foundry of John Walker which gained a national reputation. Following the manufacture of the wrought iron gates for Kew Gardens in 1846, John Walker was appointed Ironfounder to the queen, and therefore royal crests were sometimes put onto his ironwork. His biggest commission followed – to make the railings around the British Museum. These were installed in 1852 and still survive to this day. The railways were also a natural outlet for iron products and his work included railings, gates and even railway coaches. Although the clients were mostly local the growth of the British Empire led to orders in India for a 'massive quantity of magnificent iron pallisading with large gates' to enclose a burial ground in Holkar and to Mauritius for gates in the Royal Botanical Gardens.

In London during 1851 the magnificent spectacle of the Great Exhibition was held in the Crystal Palace. The Exhibition set the country alight and there were organised trips from across the country. Today the only remnant of the Exhibition and the excitement it caused in York is a pub named 'The Crystal Palace' on Holgate Road.

In the next decade a resident gave a description of the streets of York which cannot have been very different to that of the 1850s

> The streets are filled with 'slow moving heavy carts and wagons … Towering above this moving mass … is a multitude of omnibuses, vans and wagonettes drawn by two, three or four horses'. Also in this scene were the carriages of the wealthy and a mêlée of farm animals 'sheep by the score or hundred, with horned cattle, bewildered and terror struck, rushing headlong between the wheels, amongst the horses legs, starting back from one carriage only to rush against another'.

Add to this the dismay of ladies and timid persons and the scene of chaotic life in the streets of York is complete.

RELIGION IN 1851

The second census of 1851 was the religious census, called the Census of Religious Worship. The results revealed that about 10,000 adults worshipped in Anglican churches, which equated to approximately thirty-seven per cent of York's population. A challenge faced by the Church of England was the expansion of the city into newly built suburbs and to cater for the increased population new churches were built, such as St Paul's Holgate Road (in 1856) and churches out at the nearby villages of Clifton and Heworth. Even though there were wide variations in attendance – with the wealthier parishes of Micklegate having almost double the number of the poor Walmgate parishes, it is still an impressive figure and equalled about half of the total adult worshipping population of York.

There were challengers to the Anglican supremacy from two different directions. The first was the dissenting churches who had formed their own churches and organisations, breaking away from the Church of England. These churches included the Wesleyans, Independents (also known as Congregationalists) and Presbyterians. Their fortunes varied – between the early 1830s and 1862 there was no Baptist chapel in the city – whilst the Independent churches had approximately nine per cent of the worshipping adult population. However, it was the Wesleyans who eclipsed the other dissenting churches with fourteen per cent of adult worshippers and on the day of the census nearly 1,500 people were recorded as attending the magnificent new Centenary Chapel in St Saviourgate which had been completed in 1840. The attendance of Wesleyans that day was greater than every other church, including the Minster.

A small but increasingly powerful dissenting group were the Society of Friends, or Quakers. The Quakers had a powerful reforming agenda and were heavily involved in health and social reform.

Perhaps surprisingly in the city where there were twenty-three Anglican churches, not including the Church of St Peter (increasingly known as the Minster), the Roman Catholic church prospered. Catholics had been tolerated and whilst not actively encouraged could hold important positions. The Bar Convent nunnery lay just beyond Micklegate Bar and a Catholic Lord Mayor was appointed in 1830. However antagonism against the Catholic population hardened following the immigration of the poverty stricken Irish who had fled their country as a result of the potato famine. Initially the Roman Catholic diocese was at Beverley, but with the huge new Irish populations in the industrial towns a new diocese was created in Leeds, and another in Middlesbrough. The dividing line was the River Ouse and therefore the Catholics of York were divided between two dioceses.

George Hudson – The Railway King

George Hudson was one of the great railway pioneers of the nineteenth century and at one point controlled thousands of miles of track. He was born at Howsham in the East Riding on 10 March 1800. Although he came from a reasonably wealthy family, George was the youngest son of the family who had to make his own way in the world. He came to York and worked in a drapers shop in College Street near the Minster. It was there he met his future wife, Elizabeth Nicholson and he married at the age of twenty-one in 1821. They were to have seven children.

Then Hudson had a stroke of luck as he inherited a substantial legacy of £27,000. With his windfall Hudson moved rapidly up in the world. He moved to a large house in Monkgate, invested in the North Midland Railway and then built a railway linking York with towns in the West Riding. The sums of money needed for such ventures was

George Hudson, one the great railway pioneers

vast. He raised the colossal sum of £446,000 and the line was completed in May 1839.

Hudson branched out into a large number of other railway projects, though many had shady dealings. The line from York to Newcastle was a politically sensitive one and Hudson only successfully completed it by giving substantial bribes to key individuals. Another line from the Midlands to Scotland required Hudson to promise an unrealistically high dividend of six per cent in order to get the investment. By such promises he raised over five million pounds for the project.

With wealth and prestige Hudson also began to climb up the political ladder in York. In successive years he was a councillor (1835), alderman (1836) and then lord mayor in 1837, and he led the Conservative Party in the city. In 1845 he was elected Conservative MP for Sunderland, where he had substantial business interests. He used his position as MP to argue strongly in the House of Commons that the railways should not be put under government supervision

His personal connections stretched throughout the establishment. He advised Wellington, who was the prime minister and hero of Waterloo, when to buy and sell shares, and Hudson became a close friend of the famous pioneer of the railways, George Stephenson. They went into partnership and opened ironworks and coalmines. Gradually however Stephenson became suspicious of Hudson's dealings and resigned from their partnership.

Although Hudson was phenomenally wealthy on paper, largely on account of the inflated prices of railway shares, he was using up his capital at an alarming rate. He often tried dubious methods to undermine rivals and he spent £80,000 unsuccessfully opposing a rival's plans for a rail link between York and London. The great promises made by Hudson and others about the railway investments had driven share prices ever higher during the 1840s. By the middle of the decade Hudson's companies owned 1,106 miles of track and had personally invested £319,835 in railway shares. He was called 'The Railway King'.

The lure of wealth and continuing his plans had meant that Hudson had used inside information to manipulate share prices. This ploy was initially very successful, but, in 1847, investor confidence waned and share prices fell sharply. At this point Hudson's fortunes collapsed. A parliamentary committee exposed Hudson's dealings. These included his inflated promises to investors, bribing MPs and selling land he did not own. To his credit, Hudson admitted his offences and agreed to pay back money to investors. Even so, those with large amounts of railway stock faced bankruptcy. Not surprisingly much of the anger was turned against Hudson. He himself faced ruin and had to resign his positions on numerous railway boards. To escape his debtors he fled to France, but on his return, aged sixty-five, he was imprisoned in York Castle debtors prison. His friends bailed him out and from them he lived in quiet retirement in London until his death on 14 December 1871. His body was brought back to Yorkshire and is buried in the family grave at Scrayingham. His wife died in 1886.

THE GROWTH OF THE RAILWAY IN YORK

Even though disgraced, George Hudson's legacy was one of hundreds of miles of railway tracks, many of which passed through York. York steadily became more and more important as the daily number of trains arriving at York increased: 1854, 76 trains; 1868, 94 trains; 1878, 154 trains; 1888, 294 trains and in 1908, 352 trains. Many were goods trains, but the numbers were considerably swelled by passenger trains running from the north to London, but also holiday makers on their way to the Yorkshire coast resorts such as Scarborough. Rail travel meant that for the first time places and resorts were available for day trips to workers either at weekends or on Bank Holidays.

It was soon apparent that the first railway station, built by 1841 inside the walls, was not large enough so a new station was completed by 1877. In its day it was the largest in Britain and reflected York's importance as a railway centre. It was located outside the walls and away from the crowded dwellings in the city walls, but it was unfortunate that it obliterated a magnificent Roman cemetery. Many of the fabulous Roman tombs and finds today can be seen in the Yorkshire Museum.

Workshops were also built for the manufacture and repair of engines

York Station which opened in 1877

and carriages and by the end of the century nearly two thousand people were employed there. New housing was developed for the workers which in turn created small suburbs outside the city walls.

Bribery and Corruption: Politics in Victorian York

Elections of Members of Parliament during the eighteenth and nine-teenth century were full of shady practices and alleged underhand deals. It was only in 1872 that the Parliamentary Act was passed which made a secret ballot compulsory. Before this date voters made their choice known openly, which in turn meant that extensive efforts were made to persuade voters to support a particular candidate. The most obvious way was for candidates to bribe voters and so the richer the candidate the more people he could influence. The practice was denounced by both sides – and especially the loser – but was common. The amounts spent per voter ranged from a few pence each upwards to a pound or more. In 1859 during the Parliamentary Election it was stated that there were 'thirty voters who might be bought for £2 a head', but as the money was not spent they voted for the opponent. Other tactics included intimidation, withholding custom from shopkeepers who supported an opponent and 'Bacchanalian revelry' – i.e. helping one's cause by freely dispensing large amount of alcohol. The combination of tactics meant that voting day itself was a lively and sometimes bad tempered occasion.

After Hudson's fall the Tory party in York were ousted from power and the Liberals swept the board in both corporation and parliamentary elections. The single most important person in mid-Victorian York politics was George Leeman. Leeman became mayor in 1853 and his grip on power continued in York for decades – his third term of office as mayor was in 1870–1. Leeman also became one of the two members of parliament for York in 1865, the other being the Conservative member Sir John Henry Lowther.

Today there is little to show of the passions of Victorian politics, though some streets still have the names of the main participants: George Hudson Street; Lowther Street and Leeman Road. A statue of George Leeman still stands near the railway station.

YORK POOR LAW UNION AND WORKHOUSE

For people with skills and in regular employment standards of living in York were rising, but for the destitute, Victorian society had little sympathy. In 1834 the system of aiding the poor was changed so that parishes could unite together to form Poor Law Unions. Each Union had a workhouse for the poor and destitute.

The workhouse was meant to be a place of last resort – a place so hard and gruelling that the destitute would avoid it at all costs. However, it was an unfortunate consequence that the majority of people in a workhouse tended to be the most unfortunate or disabled of society, the old, young, injured, insane or destitute.

Initially the York workhouse in Marygate catered for ninety paupers but a new brick building was built on Huntington Road for 607 inmates. In the 1851 census for York in the workhouse there were many elderly men who had once had respectable jobs but who could no longer care for themselves: a seaman, a hotel manager, engine fitters, railway labourers or agricultural labourers.

Prospective inmates were interviewed and following acceptance were given a rough shapeless uniform to wear. If a family entered they were split up and husbands and wives were not allowed to communicate. The plan of the workhouse on Huntington Road clearly shows the separate areas for men, women, boys and girls, with separate areas also for 'male idiots', 'female idiots', infants and unmarried women. Once inside an inmate's only possessions were their uniform and a bed in a large dormitory.

However, the workhouse was not a prison and inmates could leave permanently if their luck changed. A man leaving would also take his family with him. Alternatively inmates were allowed out for short periods to look for work.

The workhouse system lasted until the 1930s but was then phased out. Today the workhouse building still stands: it is used as student accommodation.

William Etty (1787–1849) and Victorian Art

Standing in front of York Art Gallery in Exhibition Square is a statue of one of York's most famous artists. William Etty was born in York in

1787 and his father, at first a miller, became a baker of spice bread in York. Etty trained as a printer in Hull and then was taught to paint by Sir Thomas Lawrence, a famous painter of the time. Etty's early years as an artist were of financial insecurity. In 1811 he successfully got a painting into an exhibition at the Royal Academy, though with little result. He was more successful in 1820 when a painting of his at the Royal Academy was noticed by the critics. His early years of struggling were beginning to pay off. From then on his career was one of slow but upward success. In 1825 he achieved recognition by the British art establishment by being made an Academician of the Royal Academy. He took regular trips to the Continent and gained inspiration from the Italian cities of Rome and Venice.

For the next twenty years Etty continued to paint and made enough money to be financially independent. He lived in York and on his death he was given a public funeral in the city.

As well as Etty's own paintings, the Victorian public of York had a chance to see national and international art through travelling exhibitions. These were run as commercial ventures both for the entrance fee but also to increase sales of prints and copies. The price for entry was usually either six pence or one shilling. Many paintings were of reasonable, if unexceptional, quality though pictures of international fame were exhibited in York, such as Holman Hunt's *Light of the World* in 1859 which shows Christ with a lantern, and works by Landseer were popular. As well as paintings, prints and photographs, models were shown in the De Grey Rooms in St Leonards Place of the Crimean battlefields of Sebastopol, Balaklava and Inkerman. There was a careful pricing structure to ensure different classes did not mix: between 12 p.m. and 2 p.m. the cost was two shillings and between 2–4 p.m. one shilling and 7.30–9 p.m., six pence.

QUEEN VICTORIA IN YORK

Queen Victoria came to York in 1849 on her one and only official visit to the city. On reception of the invitation the queen had initially said she would not alight from her railway carriage, but simply graciously hear the address from the window. However, on the day, 28 September, the train stopped and after the queen had heard addresses from the lord mayor and the scholars of the school of St Peters, Queen Victoria and Prince Albert walked to the Banqueting Room for a meal. The station had been extensively decorated with flags and foliage. There was considerable excitement in York about the arrival and a crowd of twenty thousand people had turned up for the event. The visit was a great success and, refreshed, the royal party continued on their way to Scotland.

The queen was a regular visitor to York as she and the household passed through on the train when she went to her Scottish estates. Her visits ended after 1861 (that year marked the death of Prince Albert and she went into mourning), but in all she visited the city eighteen times and had eaten at the station eleven times.

BREWING, PUBS AND DRINK

Brewing in taverns and the home had been traditional across England since the Middle Ages and the Victorians carried on the tradition. In the late eighteenth century there had been sixteen small brewhouses in York, but by the middle of the nineteenth century some of the breweries had amalgamated into larger firms. Many of them also owned public houses and so could sell beer directly.

With drink readily available, and few restrictions on consumption, the effects of alcohol nationally were causing considerable concern because of the social effects. These included not only drunkenness and violence, but also the authorities saw that the poor often spent the little money they had in the numerous pubs and taverns.

In 1831 the Temperance Society was formed in Bradford and quickly spread to other cities. The Society promoted total abstinence from alcohol and it was a powerful counter to the culture of alcohol. However, despite the Temperance Society's best efforts the amount of alcohol brewed in the city increased and the pub remained a focus of community life.

The Quakers also saw the terrible effects of alcohol and attempted to offer alternatives in the form of chocolate drinks. The Rowntree and Terry families – both Quakers – started chocolate businesses in York. In Birmingham the Quaker Cadbury family also set up a chocolate factory and in the earliest days members of the Rowntree and Cadbury families were close friends. Chocolate was a favourite business commodity for pacifist Quaker businessmen both for its nutritional value and as an alternative to the manufacture of weapons.

LAW AND ORDER

Alcohol does not automatically lead to riotous behaviour, but the possibility was constantly on the minds of the city authorities. At the beginning of the nineteenth century drunkenness and prostitution were common complaints and the 'very great disorder' which happened nightly on York streets was thought to be because the pubs had no closing times so beggars could drink as long as they liked. The system of constables who only worked during the day was inadequate for the growing city.

The response was twofold: citizens set up their own clubs to tackle lawlessness such as the York Society for the Prosecution of Felons and the gloriously named York Society for the Prevention and Discouragement of Vice and Profaneness. Later in the century there was also the York Society for the Prevention of Youthful Depravity. The corporation also took measures which included appointing a police officer with two assistants in the 1820s, and later nine policemen patrolled the city at night.

In 1836 a unified police force was created, which consisted of only twelve men, William Pardoe as superintendent, an inspector and ten constables. Throughout the century the police force in York and nationally became increasingly professional. The number of tasks they had to do rapidly grew, thereby requiring a larger force. By 1855 the force had grown to thirty men, including the first detective in York and by 1893 105 men were employed as policemen.

LITERATURE

In the Victorian period there is no great literature associated with York. Elsewhere the Industrial Revolution had stirred the passions of writers who wrote about the 'Condition of England' which contrasted the poverty and hardship of some with the wealth and privilege of others.

Whilst York was not the home of any writer of national importance, the city had two literary associations. The first was Charles Dickens.

Dickens visited York a total of four times and his brother, Alfred Lambert Dickens, lived in the city for some years. Also working for the firm that Alfred worked for was one Richard Chicken, a highly eccentric character who was the inspiration for one of Dickens' most memorable characters, Mr Micawber, in the novel *David Copperfield*. It was the fictional Mr Micawber – and possibly the real Richard Chicken – who uttered the lines

> Annual income twenty pounds, annual expenditure nineteen nineteen six, result happiness,
> Annual income twenty pounds, annual expenditure twenty pounds and six, result misery.

Dickens' first visit was in 1838 on his way to investigate the appalling conditions of some Yorkshire boarding schools, the results of which he used in his novel *Nicholas Nickleby* which was finished a year later. During his first visit Dickens was shown round the Minster by his York friend Dr Camidge and the novelist particularly admired the Five Sisters window.

Dickens visited York on three further occasions, twice in 1858 and once in 1869 and each time in the city he gave one of his legendary readings. On his first 1858 visit he read *A Christmas Carol* which received excellent reviews with a local newspaper describing it as a mixture of a 'parlour reading and a stage recitation'. His last visit in 1869 was billed as 'the last Mr Dickens will give in York', a true prophecy as he died in June 1870.

A more tentative connection that York has to literary greatness is that of Anne Brontë. Anne was governess at Thorpe Green Hall in Thorpe Underwood about fifteen miles from York. The Brontë sisters, Charlotte, Emily and Anne, lived in the bleak Pennine village of Haworth, and their home, the parsonage, is today open to visitors. The novels of the three sisters are some of the masterpieces of Victorian literature, with Charlotte writing *Jane Eyre* and Emily writing *Wuthering Heights*. Anne's novels are less well known but include *Agnes Grey* and *The Tenant of Wildfell Hall*. In 1849 Anne fell ill and in order to take the sea air she travelled to Scarborough. On her way she stayed in Coney Street, in the heart of York. She died at Scarborough and is buried there.

Yorkshire Divided, 1888

In 1888 the old county of Yorkshire was divided into three separate counties, of West Riding, North Riding and East Riding, each with their own county halls, prisons and offices. The centres of each were, respectively, Wakefield, Northallerton and Beverley which have remained to this day. However, there was a huge disparity between the populations of the Ridings: whilst the East and North Ridings each had between 300,000 and 350,000 in 1881, the West Riding had 2,165,056 people within its boundaries. Whereas the North and East Ridings had four county or municipal boroughs each, the West Riding had twenty, which included the major industrial cities of Leeds (the fifth largest city in England) and Sheffield (the seventh largest city), along with Bradford and Wakefield. Leeds was three times as big as York, Sheffield over twice as big, and Bradford just under twice as big. From being the most important town in the north in the Middle Ages, the vast sprawling, giant, industrial towns of the West Riding had far exceeded York's size and economic influence, a disparity which continued to grow through the Victorian era.

ARCHITECTURE

The expansion of the city during the Victorian era resulted in many new and fine buildings around the city. The buildings in Clifford Street not only show a range of Victorian styles, but also how the buildings have since been transformed into different uses. A once fine chapel has been gutted and turned into the fire station; the magistrate's court – with turrets and a very useful clock – has continued its original purpose of law enforcement (it used to be the old police station); and the technical college, with its fine ornate frontage, is now a nightclub and a grisly visitor attraction. Elsewhere in the city there are fine remnants of Victorian interiors: the bank building on the corner of Coney Street and New Street with its remarkable ceiling, the old Yorkshire Club in Museum Street which is now a pizza house, and the De Grey Rooms (currently the Tourist Information Centre) which was built as the mess rooms of the cavalry unit, the Yorkshire Hussars.

Many of the larger buildings in York have kept their original uses, such as the Art Gallery (built in 1876), the chocolate factories of Rowntree's (now owned by Nestlé) and Terry's (closure announced 2004) and the railway station and administrative building. When first built the station was the largest in the world, thereby showing York's significance for the country's rail network.

THE END OF AN ERA, 1901

Queen Victoria died in 1901 and the nation went into mourning. Victoria had reigned longer than any other monarch in English history: it was the passing of an era. During her reign York had grown substantially and become more of an industrialised town. The notion of the British Empire had increasingly become a reality, with territorial gains for the British around the world, and particularly in Africa. In York this was reflected both in the classroom with the creation of Empire Day, when the Empire was celebrated, and also in the military with soldiers from York fighting in the Boer war and the growth of the barracks in Fulford. Goods from across the world were becoming more familiar and stories of daring adventurers were made available through the creation of the public library – the impetus for which was to celebrate the fiftieth year of Queen Victoria's reign.

CHAPTER EIGHT

York in the Twentieth Century

A Snapshot of York

In 1901 Queen Victoria died after the longest reign in English history. The country, and York, had undergone profound changes. York had continued to grow at a fast rate throughout the Victorian era and continued to do so into the twentieth century. With the exception of three decades, York's population grew between 10 per cent and 15 per cent every decade: in 1841 there were 28,842 people living in York, in 1901 67,004 people (though the boundary had been enlarged) and in 1951 there were 105,371 people.

However, whilst many cities had grown as fast, or faster, and all had areas of slums, what makes York unique is the survey of living conditions published by Seebohm Rowntree in 1901. Seebohm was a member of the wealthy and powerful Quaker family who owned Rowntree's chocolate. He was also passionately interested in the plight of the poor. For the first time Rowntree systematically noted and classed all of the population into different economic groups. Rowntree discovered that over a quarter (27.8 per cent) of the population were living in primary or secondary poverty and for the poorest in society the most popular pastime was visiting the pub. Along five hundred yards of Walmgate and Fossgate there were twenty pubs, four off licences and a club. Rowntree also noted a common sight – of women in the Irish areas sitting smoking pipes on the kerb outside their cottages.

To escape the noise and bustle of the city the more prosperous moved beyond the city walls into the leafier suburbs. This class often hired servants who lived in the same house. In between the poor and the wealthy were those who were reasonably well off and lived in specially built houses around their work places, whether near the railway or the larger factories such as the Rowntree factory on Haxby Road. Within York the city had many shopkeepers and prosperous artisans who further added to the overall wealth of the city.

For people who could afford to go to entertainments or events there were many that could be undertaken around 1900. Clubs in York included roller-skating, cycling, amateur dramatics, church clubs and choirs. In 1902 the Corn Exchange (built in 1868) was converted into the Grand Opera House which during the next decades was the home to many famous people, including Laurel and Hardy, Gracie Fields, George Formby and the ballerina Anna Pavlova. Another venue was the Assembly Rooms and in November 1900 there was grand civic ball which was described by the *Yorkshire Evening Press*. Fluted muslin of rose pink and green hung from the walls and the ends of the ballroom were luxuriously furnished with palms, foliage and comfortable seats for tired dancers.

York and the Boer War 1899–1902

In 1899 the struggle for control of South Africa between the Dutch and English settlers erupted into all out war. At the time it was considered to be one of the most terrible wars ever fought by the British because the Dutch guerrilla commandos used 'hit and run' tactics on the cumbersome British army.

As a garrison town York experienced the rise in military activity as troops were mobilised and shipped overseas. The men and women of Yorkshire suffered a high price and the County memorial to those who died stands near York Minster. It records the 1,490 people who lost their lives – including two female nurses who served in the campaign. The actual range of causes of death is large, but the number killed by disease (764) was over twice that killed by the enemy (354). The single greatest period of death for the Yorkshire regiments was during the Bloemfontein campaign where typhoid struck, causing the soldiers to nickname the place 'Blooming-typhoid-town'.

Despite the great hardships that the soldiers faced in South Africa, many could not find employment when they returned. Some were so poverty stricken that they had to sell or pawn furniture and in some cases even their wedding rings. At the unveiling ceremony of the memorial on 3 August 1905 many soldiers had no medals to wear as they had been forced to sell them.

TRANSPORT

By the turn of the century the motor car was slowly becoming a familiar site in the city, though the usual form of transport was horse drawn vehicles or trams. As today, cars and horses did not always mix and it was 'the passage of a swift-travelling motor-car' that caused the retired policeman, Superintendant Dove, to be thrown from his trap in Goodramgate.

Electric trams, running on a system of rails, were a familiar sight at the turn of the century and in 1909 the corporation bought the City of York Tramway Company and so took control of transport in York.

An oddity – and a solution only attempted in seven other cities in England – was the battery operated bus, or the 'Electrobus'. As no independent operator could be found the corporation decided to run them themselves, though it needed an act of Parliament to do so. It proved to be a short lived experiment as the first was bought in 1915 and the last was sold in 1923.

Traffic congestion has always been a serious issue in the narrow and winding streets of York, with the crossing of the rivers being particularly problematic. Ouse Bridge had, since Viking times, been the main route across the river. The current bridge was completed in 1820 and was paid for by a series of loans, money from the corporation and tolls. The last tolls were levied in 1829. Lendal Bridge was newly built and was completed in 1863. The third, and final, city centre bridge to be built was Skeldergate Bridge, which was completed in 1881. Tolls were levied on traffic to help finance the scheme and were only abolished on 1 April 1914.

SPORT

During the late nineteenth century rugby was the dominant game in York, although there were a wide range of other sports clubs, whether cricket, football, bowling or cycling. Swimming was also encouraged by the opening of open air municipal baths in the 1870s.

Gradually football became more popular than rugby and cup competitions were organised, along with a Schools League. Teams were formed from a wide range of organisations, including workers from the Rowntree's factory (who were one of the better sides in York), church sides, such as the Hungate Mission, and various army sides: York and Lancaster Regiment, 5th Royal Irish Lancers and the Border Regiment.

The first York club, the York City Football Club, was formed in 1908 and had a ground in Holgate Road which had two stands. The larger stand was canvas-covered, could hold three hundred people and came from York Racecourse. In 1912 the club was admitted into the Midland League and a new ground, at Field View, was opened. For the opening match there were five thousand paying spectators, with ladies being admitted free.

The club survived in the League until the start of the First World War in 1914 which resulted in suspending the League. The end for the club came quickly. In 1917 a creditor forced the club into liquidation, its assets including the stands were sold off and the ground, Field View, was turned into allotments and then a housing estate. It was another five years before a club called York City rose from the ashes.

York in the First World War

York, like every other town in England, was caught up in the initial enthusiasm for the First World War and many men joined the Services. A huge army camp was constructed on the Knavesmire for soldiers and cavalry to prepare for the war. Recruiting officers toured the city enlisting men for the army. Throughout the war numerous new units were formed of men from York and Yorkshire, for example in 1915 210 men formed the 144 Heavy Battery of Royal Garrison Artillery. The unit went to the front in January 1916.

As York contained a military garrison, the army's presence was highly noticeable in the city with large numbers of men in uniforms.

Those who were not in uniform were considered to be conscientious objectors and the mood against them was such that women were urged to cross over the road to avoid them or they were given white feathers as a sign of cowardice.

Within the city the citizens did the best they could for the soldiers and sailors who passed through. A canteen was set up on York station supplying tea and refreshments to travelling service men, and the Assembly Rooms became a supper, bed and breakfast station for stranded service men.

THE ZEPPELIN AIR RAIDS 1916

The air war, compared to later periods, was practically non-existent, but a series of three air raids by Zeppelin airships brought the reality of war home to the citizens of York during 1916. The first attack, on 2 May 1916, caught the authorities and citizens completely unaware. There were no defences against air attack and the Zeppelin had a free passage across York. It dropped bombs to the south of the city (in Nunthorpe Avenue), which killed one person and injured another, then across the centre of York and onto Peaseholme Green where a series of bombs caused the most deaths and injury. After the raid there was considerable public outrage and defences, in the form of ack-ack guns and searchlights were installed at strategic points.

These were in place for the second and third raids which took place on 25 September 1916 and the night of the 27–28 November 1916. During the second raid the searchlights and guns made it uncomfortable for the airship which tried to manoeuvre out of the way. The most serious damage was to Heworth Church when a bomb landing nearby blew out all the windows.

The third attack was part of a much bigger German aerial assault. Ten airships left Germany for different targets across England. The raids were a disaster, with two Zeppelins shot down, two turned back and six failed to cause much damage. The Zeppelin which attacked York was quickly picked up by searchlight. The airship was hit and rapidly lost height. To lessen its weight it dropped its bombs. Most fell harmlessly, but some hit houses in Haxby Road and nearby Fountayne Street causing a few deaths.

The unsuccessful raids of the night of the 27–28 November were the last major Zeppelin attacks on England. However, also on the 28 November a new era dawned when a German plane launched an air raid on London.

THE LAST YEARS OF THE WAR

As the war progressed the conditions became more and more difficult. The German U Boats in the Atlantic were causing heavy losses in Allied shipping, with the result that food and other basic items could not be imported. Food rationing became more and more stringent, and each new ration was announced through a Food Control Order. In 1917 one such Order dictated a 'meatless day' and Wednesday was chosen as the day when meat could not be served in York pubs, hotels and inns. Potato less days were more common and the only days potatoes could be eaten were Wednesdays and Fridays. In the same year the highly successful 'Eat Less Bread Campaign' was launched to preserve meagre stocks of raw ingredients.

With the exceptionally heavy losses during the war there were successive attempts to conscript more and more men, either by lessening the medical standards exempting men or by raising the age of conscription. By 1917 the *Herald* newspaper estimated that between five and eight thousand men had been conscripted from York, excluding soldiers in the garrison. One result of so many men leaving for the war was that women were employed to do the work formerly undertaken by men, whether working in factories or driving lorries and buses. The previously high unemployment rates in York before the war were reversed to full employment.

The war ended on the 11 November 1918 (Armistice Day) and in York formal celebrations were held for Victory and Peace Day on the 19 July 1919. A whole series of events were organised for July and August. There was a major service in the Minster on 19 July 1919 to give formal thanks for peace, but there was also a lot of entertainments, including: folk dances; an aquatic festival and water carnival; bands; prizes for the best dressed boat, and a competition for 'walking the greasy pole in comic costume'.

In York, out of a population of 82,282 in 1911, 1,441 men and two women were killed and countless were injured, either physically or psychologically. *The King's Book of York Fallen Heroes* lists the dead and includes photographs of all but nineteen of the victims. The human dimension of the tragedy can be seen in the many war memorials around the city.

One poignant memorial is in Holy Trinity Micklegate church which commemorates the Walker family. The father, Captain Walker of the 15th Hussars, died at the age of eighty-one in 1919, having witnessed the death of all four of his sons. His third son was accidentally killed before the war in a race. His eldest two sons were both in the army and were both killed in the first year of the war in 1914. His final son was killed in the very last month of the war in November 1918. The memorial was erected by his sole remaining child, Dorothy, after the rest of her family had died.

TB and the Spanish Flu Epidemic 1918

As the First World War, or the Great War as it was known, came to a close, a great epidemic of Spanish Influenza swept across Europe. Before and during the First World War one of the most common diseases was tuberculosis (TB). TB had been an ever present danger since Victorian times in York and had increased during the war. Many soldiers and sailors returning from the war suffered from TB and campaigns were instigated to rid the city of the disease by improving hygiene and demolishing slums.

Whilst TB was a constant threat, Spanish Flu hit the city in two severe outbreaks in 1918. The first was in July and spread rapidly through York. Many school children became ill, as did twelve of the twenty Minster choristers. The second period was more serious and longer lasting, from October 1918 to January 1919. The outbreak was so severe that all schools and places of entertainment were closed and soldiers were drafted in to help dig graves. In all three hundred people died, with the outbreak in July killing thirty-three people, and the winter outbreak killing 267.

The Inter-War Years

YORK CITY FOOTBALL CLUB REBORN 1922

On 6 September 1922 a new York City Football Club played their first game, against Nottingham County Reserves, losing 4–2. The foundation of the club was built upon a growing interest in football in York with three clubs in particular taking part in the Yorkshire League – Acomb WMC(Working Men's Club), Rowntree's and York YMCA (Young Men's Christian Association).

In the first few years York City had a somewhat nomadic existence. For the first few matches the ground at Heslington Lane was not ready, so matches were played on the Rowntree's ground in Haxby Road.

THE GENERAL STRIKE, 1926

In early May 1926 a general strike was called by the Trades Union Congress (TUC) in order to support the coal miner's against the employers. However, as the TUC feared that revolutionary elements would take advantage of the situation, only key trades and workers were called out on strike. The effect was patchy with some towns and cities being paralysed by pickets whilst other places escaping relatively lightly.

In York the call to strike was loyally obeyed by virtually all the transport workers, engineers, printers and building workers, and a subsequent tally revealed that 7,032 men went on strike. Flash points in York were when pickets attempted to disrupt trains by blocking level crossings, the movement of goods, or stop buses running. However, despite strong forces of pickets there was little serious trouble in York. During the whole of the nine day strike there were only nine police summoneses made against pickets and after the resolution of the strike the industrial relations between workers and employers quickly calmed down once again.

CHOCOLATE AND RAILWAYS

At the turn of the twentieth century York was dominated by two industries: chocolate and the railways. The chocolate makers included Rowntree, Terry's and a host of smaller firms such as Cravens. It was these manufacturers who progressively expanded, especially between the First and Second World Wars. In the census of 1901 chocolate makers employed 1,994 people and by 1939 this figure had risen to 12,274. Many of these jobs were given to women and girls and if the men of the household worked there was often sufficient income to raise households out of poverty.

The second great industry was that of the railways. Ever since the days of George Hudson the railway had had a powerful presence in York, both as a major stop on the London/Edinburgh line serving Yorkshire, but also as a manufacturing and repair base. The railway employed nearly six thousand men, though by 1900 it had reached its fullest extent and kept to that level until the middle of the century.

THE CHANGING APPEARANCE OF THE CITY

During the nineteenth century some of the worst slums had been demolished, in particular the Water Lanes leading down to the Ouse. This was, however, a pin-prick for what was needed. An assessment of housing at the turn of the nineteenth century concluded that there were 1,519 slum houses in the city.

In the first half of the twentieth century there were two major developments associated with housing in the city. The first was the revolutionary concept behind the planning of New Earswick, funded by the Rowntree family and the second was the major slum clearances that took place between the end of the First World War and the Second World War.

The Quaker businessman, Joseph Rowntree, led the way to provide good affordable housing for his workers. In 1901 Rowntree purchased 123 acres of land and by 1904 thirty houses had been built, let at a very reasonable five shillings a week. The houses were well built, with good sanitation in spacious surroundings. It was a pioneering move and this development, and others like it, were the forerunners of the Garden City movement, which reacted against the conditions of grim industrial cities to create a spacious and green environment. Welwyn Garden City in Hertfordshire still preserves this concept within its name.

The start of the major improvements in housing by the corporation came between the First World War and the Second World War. The city authorities in particular concentrated on two slum areas within Walmgate and Hungate. Surveys of the city had shown that at the turn of the century up to twenty-five houses might share a single water tap in the poorer parts of York, and outside toilets were commonly shared between households.

These areas contained slums which at their worst had harboured appalling conditions and disease. Between 1919 and 1939 1,908 houses were demolished, over five thousand new council houses were built and seven thousand people were re-housed. New estates with tree lined avenues were built for residents outside the city walls in Acomb, Tang Hall, Heworth and Holgate. However, what replaced the old slum areas was sometimes not an improvement and in the case of Hungate ugly light industrial units were built. Slowly the city was becoming a place of work and was dying in the evenings.

One major visual change which occurred in 1935 was the destruction of the external walls of the castle area. Today view of Clifford's Tower is unhindered, but before 1935 there were thirty-five foot high walls surrounding the castle. The walls were awesome in their scale and appearance, not only from their height, but they were also made of blackened mill-stone grit.

EMPLOYMENT

Between the wars there was also a social shift in employment nationally and within York. By the start of the First World War in 1914 80 per cent of women were domestic servants in York, but thereafter domestic servants steadily declined in number as the social and economic circumstances of households changed. Women were increasingly employed in offices and factories either as secretaries to male managers or on the conveyor belts of factories such as Rowntrees.

The Second World War

PREPARATIONS

War was declared by Britain upon Germany on Sunday, 3 September 1939. As the storm clouds of war drew ever darker on the Continent,

York prepared for war. On the home front black out curtains were put up, stirrup pumps acquired to put out small fires and tape was put onto windows to stop flying glass if they were shattered by bomb blasts.

Within the city the preparations were extensive and involved. Air raid shelters were either constructed in people's back gardens, or public shelters were set up around York. Around the city there were huge static water tanks to supply water in case of bombing. One stood on the ground outside the east end of All Saint's Pavement and formed a roundabout in the road. Others were to have huge implications for the archaeology of York. Huge water tanks were dug beside the Minster in Dean Park in case of an air raid. The scale of these tanks can still be seen today as a slight rise in the level of the lawns in Dean Park. In times of war careful archaeological excavation was not considered and it is unfortunate that the tanks were probably dug in one of the most archaeologically sensitive areas in the whole of York. Modern research has shown that the tanks have probably destroyed the evidence for the Anglo-Saxon and Viking Minsters. Whether anything survives will be a question only the archaeologists can discover in the future.

THE MILITARY IN YORK

On a military footing York was the headquarters for the army's Northern Command. The West Yorkshire Regiment was based at Fulford Barracks, which was renamed Imphal Barracks in honour of the regiment's action in Burma, where the key Manipur Valley was held against the Japanese and so saved India from invasion.

The headquarters for Group 4 Bomber Command was in Heslington Hall, a Tudor house just outside the city. In both July 1941 and February 1942 Group 4 had 153 operational and thirty-eight non-operational bombers whilst in December 1943 it commanded 205 operational Halifax bombers. In 1943 airfields commanded from Heslington included those at Snaith, Pocklington, Holme on Spalding Moor and, close to the city, at Elvington. In 1944 Elvington had the distinction of being the home to the only two French heavy-bomber squadrons to join Bomber Command – Nos. 346 and 347 Squadrons and by September 1944 the station was commanded by an officer of the French Air Force and had French personnel. After the war, in 1955, a fine astronomical clock was installed in York Minster in memory of the airmen who lost their lives in the war.

York's factories were also converted to help the war effort. The assembly line workers at Rowntree switched from making chocolate to making munitions, and the workers regularly made over 160,000 shells a week. At Terry's chocolate factory propeller blades were made.

Unlike the First World War, in the Second World War unmarried women between twenty and thirty were conscripted as well as men, though not for the front line. Many women joined the Land Army and worked on the farms around York – a novel and tiring experience for many city women. Many men who continued to work in the city joined the Local Defence Volunteers, known as the Home Guard which were used to watch for enemy attack or guard strategic points. On clear nights bombing raids on the docks at Hull could be seen.

1942 AIR RAID

The civilian population of York did not escape the effects of the Second World War. There were several air raids, though there was only one serious air raid upon the city when, on the night of 29 April 1942, the German Luftwaffe launched a raid on York. One explanation is that it was part of a bombing campaign across England known as the 'Baedeker Raids' which were supposedly in retaliation for the RAF raids on German historic cities and were so called because the Luftwaffe chose their targets from the Baedeker tourist guides of England. However, York was also a major railway terminus which served the ports of the East coast, was on the main route from London to Edinburgh and had significant railway yards, with associated railway engine manufacturing and repair.

The raid caused significant death and damage with eighty-seven deaths and many more injuries. If the main target was the railway station it was successful as it was virtually destroyed, and there was also damage across large parts of the city, including the destruction of the medieval Guildhall on Coney Street and the nearby church of St Martin Le Grand. On the domestic front 9,500 houses were damaged. Amazingly the Minister remained unscathed.

THE HOME FRONT

Life in the city during the war was often hard. Large numbers of men had joined the army leaving their wives to cope with the children. This was made harder by the scarcity of food. Food rationing started in 1940 and became progressively more rigorous. Weekly rations included roughly one pound of meat, eight ounces of cheese, eight ounces of fat, eight ounces of sugar and four ounces of jam. It was not surprising that people tried to supplement their rations and for those with access to the countryside there were rabbits, fruits and bird eggs at various times of the year. Whale meat was also occasionally available and to supplement real eggs and milk there was the powdered variety – powdered eggs in particular were loathed by many. Clothing was also rationed and a 'points' system was used – a year's worth of points equated to one outfit.

The fear of German bombers also resulted in strict blackouts being imposed. No light was allowed to come from houses – the Air-Raid Precautions (ARP) Warden's famous phrase was 'Put that light out' – and there were no street lights. At first vehicles could not even have headlights, but so many accidents followed that they were eventually allowed a thin pencil of light. On an overcast night walking round York was difficult and many cartoons made fun of the painful experience of falling down a pot hole.

However, it wasn't all doom and gloom. There was a constant round of dances and entertainments put on for the troops, dance halls and there were ten cinemas in the city which showed regular newsreels of how the war was progressing.

At 7.30 p.m. on 7 May 1945 'Victory in Europe' (VE Day) was announced and there were instantaneous parties in the city. Flags were hung out and people danced in the streets.

Post-World War II – 1945–1960

In the immediate aftermath of the war, conditions actually worsened for a time. The demobilisation of soldiers from the forces meant that many were unemployed. The barracks at York was the north of England's centre for demobilisation of troops. Rationing not only continued but got worse and in 1948 bread and potatoes were rationed for the first time. However over the next six years rationing was systematically abolished on all items. Meat rationing was the last to go in 1954.

National politics had a considerable effect on York. In the General Election of 1945 the Labour Party won a landslide victory promising great changes. Many industries, such as the railways and the coal mines were nationalised and brought into public ownership. This included the railway assets based in York and the coal mines around Selby, to the south of York, were similarly affected. However, the greatest change was the creation of the National Health Service. Previously people had personally paid doctors when they visited – now health care was free at the point of delivery.

THE FESTIVAL OF THE ARTS, 1951

In 1951 a nationwide Festival of the Arts was organised, to 'challenge the sloughs of the present' and so cast forth 'a shaft of confidence ... against the future'. The fact that 1951 was also the centenary of perhaps the most memorable exhibition ever held in England – the Great Exhibition of 1851 – was not lost on the organisers either. The main centres were London, Glasgow and Cardiff, but there were also twenty-two provincial centres. The majority of the provincial centres were in the south and York was the centre for the whole of the north of England, with its nearest challenger being Liverpool.

The York authorities concentrated on two elements. The first was the staging of the Mystery Plays for the first time since 1580. The plays were a real community event and York's amateur dramatic societies supplied the majority of the three hundred strong cast. Only Jesus was played by a professional actor, Joseph O'Connor.

The other, more surprising event, was the architectural competition and building of new flats on Paragon Street, the Festival Flats. Although not inspiring to look at by today's standards, in 1951 it was hoped that they would provide a link between the year and the future. The final outcome was a series of flats which were described by the local press as 'outstanding in design' and a 'modern architectural highlight'. There was considerable interest in the flats during the festival and over 1,300 visited them to look over their interiors.

However, it was the Mystery Plays which were the focus of the festival drawing in crowds from a wide area. They were held outdoors in the setting of St Mary's Abbey and fortunately the rain held off for most of the performances. They were hailed as a triumph, being described as 'one of the most exciting experiences … the Festival has yet to offer in the way of live performances'.

The restarting of the tradition of performing the Mystery Plays is perhaps the greatest legacy of the Festival of the Arts in 1951, for the tradition continues to this day in York.

THE 1960s

During the 1950s and 1960s Europe and America witnessed an explosion of music and popular culture after the austerity of the immediate post-war years. The atmosphere of the times was to banish the past and look only to the present or the future, whether in fashion, music or building. The term 'teen age' was coined in America where it was first used in an advertisement which claimed that adolescents were 'living in the "teen age"' and it captured the mood of youth and change. In England there were two main *foci* – London for fashion (especially in the Carnaby Street area) and avant garde thinking (based in the London School of Economics – the LSE), and in Liverpool for music, with arguably one of the greatest bands of all time – The Beatles – originating from there.

The post-war social changes swirling around the country also affected York and new bands and dance venues opened up. The two biggest names in music entertainment in York were the Rialto and the Empire. The Rialto in particular played host to some of the great names of the era, including the Rolling Stones, Jerry Lee Lewis, Tommy Steele and Frankie Vaughan.

ARCHITECTURE

The demand for change affected many areas of life and the most visible was the change in architecture. Around the country the historic heart of cities were torn apart in the belief that the architecture of the past was of no consequence. In Coventry more significant properties were torn down in the 1960s than had been damaged by wartime bombing.

York was largely spared the blight of horrendous 1960s architecture, though some was built. The belief system behind the new architecture was that communal life and new thought could lead to a revolution in the society that would benefit all.

Whilst the ideas might be fascinating, the buildings are often disliked and visually horrible to look at. In York the largest scale project in the town centre was that of the Stonebow complex. In its design the architect's vision can be seen, with a curving shape mirroring the road, which is counter-balanced by the soaring vertical line of the main tower. That said, it is out of scale and does not fit at all into the historic heart of the city. The city authorities are to be praised that this is the only large scale piece of 1960s ugliness that exists in York, though plenty of smaller examples exist.

UNIVERSITY

During the 1960s both Labour and Conservative governments promoted education, and especially higher education and this led to a large number of new universities being founded across the United Kingdom. The older, Victorian, universities were known collectively as 'red brick' universities from their building materials and the new universities had so many windows in that they were known as 'plate glass' universities.

The 1960s Stonebow complex

In April 1960 approval was given for the establishment of a university in York. In many respects it was remarkable that one had not emerged before, but the previous attempts to found a university in the seventeenth century and from the 1840s onwards had all foundered.

The university was founded upon the system used in both Oxford and Cambridge of having separate colleges, each with their own libraries, canteens and bars. One result of the collegiate system is that there is no central, single bar, for all students and no central student union building, a fact which may be a reason why the radical political student movements has never been a feature of York as so often as has been the case elsewhere. As with any institution the university has its own traditions and myths. A constant one is that the large Central Hall is sinking into the central lake.

One of the most pleasant features of the university is the fourteen acre central lake (unless one ended up in it, either through falling in or being thrown in) which was a previously waterlogged area. Ducks, geese and fish were introduced and it has become a haven for wildlife.

Over the generations since its beginnings the university has grown. The colleges are both growing and changing, and new colleges are being built. The university has not only become one of the top universities in the country but is also one of the three largest employers in York, alongside Nestlé (which bought up Rowntrees) and the city council itself.

Elsewhere in the city other higher educational institutions also flourish. There is a Law School which predominantly teaches conversion courses for graduates who want to enter the law, and the College of St John, which started as a Church of England teacher training college, has become affiliated to the University of Leeds.

THE RING ROAD SCHEME

In the middle years of the twentieth century the car became the vehicle of choice for millions of people, but in a city such as York there was the serious possibility of congestion through the narrow streets. A major debate started as to how best to tackle the problems and one solution – which had many powerful backers – was for a major ring road around the city close to or within the city walls. The scheme got to the planning stage and schemes were drawn up. The areas through which the road was to be bulldozed became depopulated and property prices began to plummet. Such areas included Walmgate and the now wealthy properties on the Mount. The scheme progressed to the point that one of the consultants on the project had the task of visiting the owners of houses to tell them their homes were to be bulldozed.

Gradually the implications of the transformation of the York landscape began to be evident and the outcry from the citizens of York proved to be too deafening to ignore. The scheme was eventually shelved, thereby saving the city from the worst of the ravages of the development for the car.

LORD ESHER'S REPORT, 1969

Although York survived the worst ravages of development in the 1960s there was growing concern that the historic fabric of York, and other historic cities, would be destroyed. Lord Esher was commissioned by the government to write a report about development in York. His report was ground breaking in its proposals and was a detailed and down to earth programme of conservation. One of his most important proposals was that housing should once again be built within the city walls. Previously to this the policy was of slum clearance and moving the population out to the city's suburbs. Whilst this improved living conditions the heart of the city was seen to be dying with everyone leaving at the end of the working day. Since the report there have been some large scale quality housing developments which has improved the sense that York has a living and vibrant heart at all times of day and night. Other improvements include making one of the largest pedestrian city centre areas in England and reducing the impact of the car within the centre.

THE MINSTER EXCAVATIONS 1967–72

Whilst the ring road scheme was causing consternation in the city, another serious problem was being resolved. During the mid 1960s it had become evident that the main tower of the Minster was coming away from the walls at an alarming rate. Cracks were appearing and getting ever wider. A survey was undertaken which revealed that within fifteen years the Minster would not be able to survive the repairs which were needed to save it. The situation was so serious that there was the real possibility that the central tower of the Minster would soon collapse and come crashing down onto the nave. The solution was to underpin the main tower using a system of concrete and metal rods. The required amount, two million pounds was raised through an energetic appeal.

The first stage of the process was to excavate underneath the tower. Archaeologists painstakingly removed the accumulated levels of centuries of soil to uncover the archaeology of the Minster. The single most important discovery was that the new Norman church, built by the first Norman archbishop, Thomas of Bayeux, was not built on the site of the previous Anglo-Saxon and Viking Minsters. This was a considerable surprise to archaeologists and historians alike and even today the site of the Anglo-Saxon Minster is one of speculation rather than definite proof. Below the foundations of the Norman Minster lay a Viking and Anglo-Saxon burial ground, and below them the most important Roman building in York, the *principia*.

The engineering feat to secure the Minster foundations included the installing of concrete 'collars' which were tied together by twenty thousand feet of steel rods, and the central tower was further braced by steel rods.

REORGANISATION OF 1974

In 1974 administrative reorganisation by central government took place across England and one of the cities effected was York. For centuries it had been a county borough and had control over all its local functions, but following the reorganisation North Yorkshire County Council, based in Northallerton, took over social services and education departments. York was relegated to a district council, though the queen recognised its historic importance and by charter allowed it to retain its city status, retain the post of sheriff and the chairman of the council can be called 'The Right Honourable Lord Mayor'.

THE NATIONAL RAILWAY MUSEUM 1975

The siting of the National Railway Museum in York was the first time that a national museum had been situated outside London. The move was strongly fought against by those people who wanted the museum in London, but there was great local support for the national museum. York already had a small railway museum, staffed by volunteers, and the council lent their support by approving plans and encouragement. A petition in support of the museum carrying ninety thousand signatures was delivered to the government minister responsible. The museum was finally opened in the autumn of 1975.

Today the National Railway Museum has expanded and performs the valuable task of preserving the engines, rolling stock and archives connected with the development of the railways in the British Isles. In 2001 a new government initiative to encourage access into national museums resulted in free admission.

THE COPPERGATE EXCAVATIONS AND THE JORVIK VIKING CENTRE 1976–85

During the 1970s plans had been developed to develop a shopping centre off Coppergate, which in the process demolished Cravens, one of York's smaller and less well known makers of chocolate. As a condition of developing there was an archaeological dig by York Archaeological Trust. The excavations lasted from 1976–1981 and revealed extensive remains of the Viking city, a city known to the Vikings as Jorvik. The scale and miraculous preservation of the remains took everyone by surprise and a fabulous snap shot of the Viking city emerged. The largest structures were the remains of Viking houses which stood to nearly two metres high in places. The houses had a centrally placed fire and the conditions inside would have been warm and smoky. The walls were made of two layers of timber planks which had twigs in the middle for extra insulation. Outside there were wooden planks laid down for footpaths, fences between the properties made of stout twigs, and holes in the ground used as toilets (known to archaeologists as cess pits). The remains from the cess pits reveal to archaeologists not only what people ate, but also that parasites were a common factor of life for the Vikings. The conditions within the houses were not hygienic. Archaeologists discovered rotting wood, decaying waste matter and putrid food which had often been thrown into the corners of the rooms or trampled underfoot. Add to this the fact that there would have been dogs, chickens, pigs and other animals roaming in and out of the houses and it makes for a dirty, if lively, scene.

Yet the people living in Coppergate were not poor, as objects discovered testify. Jewellery, coins and goods from abroad show a people connected with long distance trade. A silk hat was found which probably came from the Middle East, and a seashell which may have come from the Red Sea.

The excavations were a huge success, both in terms of what was discovered and the public interest. York Archaeological Trust therefore took the brave decision to recreate the Viking buildings and open it as a visitor centre. The public's response was phenomenal.

In 1984 a visit by Charles, Prince of Wales, was the formal occasion for the opening of the Jorvik Viking Centre. The project was both a leap of faith and a leap in the dark, for although the concept of a 'ride' through a scene has become popular since, at the time it was a unique venture. Since its opening it is common to see large queues eager to see the accurately recreated Viking town.

MINSTER FIRE OF 1984

On the night of 9 July 1984 a devastating blow was dealt to York Minster when a fire broke out in the roof space of the south transept caused by a lightning strike. The fire caught hold and despite fire crews being rapidly on the scene there was substantial damage. During the fire the Minster authorities had worked tirelessly in a human chain to remove the most precious portable items from the burning building. Although the roof collapsed the south wall and its priceless Rose Window were saved – just, it was estimated that a few more minutes and the wall would have collapsed.

The next morning people across the world heard of the terrible news and the citizens of York could visit the site for themselves. Gradually over the following years the south transept roof was painstakingly

York Minster burns again in July 1984

rebuilt. A competition hosted by the well known BBC Television children's programme 'Blue Peter' came up with new and often contemporary designs for the ceiling bosses. With an eye to the future one has depicted an astronaut and his, or possibly her, space ship.

FLOOD 2000

Throughout its history York has suffered from floods and a particularly bad flood had occurred in 1981, but the most recent occurred in 2000. Since the 1981 floods a new flood defence had been built which separated the Rivers Ouse and Foss. In 1981 the River Ouse had risen and its flood waters had travelled back up the River Foss causing extensive flooding along both river systems.

In 2000 heavy rain storms fell on the Yorkshire Dales and Moors which caused all the river systems which feed the River Ouse to flood. The water poured southwards and the River Ouse rose to almost unheard of levels. The city was completely reliant upon the flood defences to prevent a catastrophe. Where there are no such defences some houses were flooded causing chaos and misery but at one point the regular television reports were predicting the wholesale failure of the defences and that large areas of housing would be submerged under the flood waters. Thousands of sand bags were positioned in the danger areas. As the sun rose on the morning of Saturday 4 November there were the first signs that the water levels were beginning to drop. The mood was caught by the local newspaper, the *Evening Press*, which had a banner headline 'Great Escape' and then 'Saved! Sand Bagged City Beats Odds'.

York in the Twenty-first Century

At the start of the twenty-first century the City of York Council presides over the combination of the city centre, suburbs and countryside – in total an area of 105 square miles – and has over 181,000 residents living within its boundary. Every year the number of people in York swells with the welcome tourists who flock to the city to wonder at the Minster, attractions and the narrow medieval streets. The need to keep improving the tourism offer is itself a constant challenge and a recent innovation is the formation of the York Museums Trust which has brought together the local museums into one organisation. There is, however, a constant tension between enticing people into the city and preserving not only the historic fabric, but also taking into account the views of people already living in the city. Some issues have caused heated controversy, including the development plans for new shopping complex, known as Coppergate II, near the Castle. After many bitter arguments the plans were eventually dropped.

Whilst tourism is a vital part of the economy, the prosperity of the city cannot depend on tourism alone and so local industries are also crucial to York's wealth. However, York is part of the global economy and therefore its major industries are subject to global trading decisions – decisions which are not always in the city's interests. The major industries of York have been closed or modified. Rowntree's was bought out by Nestlé during the 1980s, and Terry's was bought out by Suchard. In May 2004 Suchard announced the closure of the Terry's factory in York. The railways too suffered with the Holgate Road railway works closing, with only a small part of the operation being bought by an American company. The York factory of the stationers and printers Ben Johnson was bought out by the American firm RR Donnelly, who later closed the factory. Many of the former industrial sites have been turned into housing developments as people wish to live within or near the attractive city centre.

A recent area of industrial expansion are the new 'high-tech' industries which have been attracted to York, because of the skills of the staff and students at the university and the educated local population generally. The Science Park has flourished with businesses being set up to capitalise on computing, physics and biological expertise.

Looking back over the whole history of York, from its Roman foundations to the present, York can be claimed by historians and archaeologists as a perfect example of each historical era since the Romans.

The foundation of the town by the Romans led to it becoming the second most important city in Roman Britain. Sections of the Legionary Fortress walls can still be seen nearly two thousand years after they were built. There is little still visible of Anglo-Saxon York though it had a key significance for the kings of Northumbria and the Minster was famed for its library. The archaeological discoveries of the Viking settlement have revealed the cultural and financial wealth of the city. The Normans then transformed the city by new building works, in particular the castles and the Minster, as well as damming the Foss. These changes have since determined the current layout of the topography of York.

However, York rose to national importance because of its strategic position close to Scotland. For a few decades York was the capital of England and as the English kings based the government in the city whilst they fought the Scots. The wealth of the medieval merchants and church in York resulted in fabulous artistic and architectural achievements, whether the rebuilding of the Minster, the stained glass in the city churches, or the Mystery Plays.

Thereafter in the following centuries York declined in national significance as London once again became the capital and other cities grew. York became a centre of regional importance in Tudor times with the King's Council of the North being based in the city, and during the Civil War it played a major role in the control of the north by either the king or parliament. During the Georgian era it became a centre of social elegance and leisure, which changed during the industrialisation of the Victorian age. In the twentieth century York survived the architectural ravages of the Second World War and the 1960s, and today its former history is the driver behind the new tourist industry.

The city has never stayed still and is still developing and changing as the new century progresses. The tensions between conservation and development to attract people and industries are likely to increase, but ultimately it is the continuity and survival of York's archaeology, buildings and records has truly made it a jewel in the history of England.

The Grand Old Duke of York

One reason that the name of York is known throughout the world is because of the nursery rhyme 'The Grand Old Duke of York'. The nursery rhyme has, of course, little to do with York itself, though there are a host of places to claim the hill in the rhyme as their own, some of which are near York. The well known children's rhyme runs:

> *The Grand Old Duke of York,*
> *He had ten thousand men,*
> *He marched them up to the top of the hill,*
> *And he marched them down again.*
> *And when they were up, they were up,*
> *And when they were down, they were down,*
> *And when they were only half way up,*
> *They were neither up nor down.*

The rhyme poses several questions to which there are no firm answers: the two main ones are 'which 'Grand Old Duke?' and 'which hill?'.

The Grand Old Duke is almost certainly Fredrick Augustus, the second son of King George III. There are two hills close to York which claim to be the location, one at the village of Crayke to the north of York and another at Allerton Park between York and Harrogate. Allerton Park has a strong claim because in 1786 it was sold to Frederick Augustus. However, so far as is known no soldiers or army were stationed there.

The most likely explanation is the rhyme either relates to the largely ineffectual troop movements around Europe, or to the time when Frederick Augustus reviewed ten thousand troops at Coxheath in Kent and required them to march up a hill to test them.

Whatever the real reason the rhyme celebrates one of the more colourful dukes of York. Frederick Augustus was wildly exuberant and extravagant: on his death he left unpaid debts of up to £500,000.

York elsewhere in the World

The name of York is associated with a variety of settlements and objects across the world, some famous in their own right and some are easily passed by. The majority are in places settled by English settlers, whether America, Canada, South Africa or Australia, though there are also other remote places called York. Today perhaps the greatest confusion between two places with York in their title are two universities, the University of York (York, England) and York University, Toronto in Canada. Both universities are highly prestigious and it is not unknown for international post to be delivered to the wrong one. The single most famous place with York as its title is, of course, New York.

New Amsterdam to New York

Initially it was the Dutch who were the first settlers in New York and its region. The initial lure was for the fur and skins found around Hudson's Bay, and gradually their presence along the coast moved southwards. The region was called New Netherland and it was formally recognised as a province in 1623. The company in charge of trade was the Dutch West India Company and in 1626 the Director General of the company, Peter Minuit, arrived and made perhaps the greatest land purchase in history, buying the island of Manhatten from the Indians for the price of a few trinkets. He immediately began to build a fort called Fort New Amsterdam. The fort and settlement was owned by the Dutch West India Company, who made the laws and appointed everyone, from doctors to lawyers to farmers.

The two main settlements were Fort New Amsterdam and Fort Orange. Fort Orange specialised in the fur trade, whilst New Amsterdam was the main trading port. Rich merchants saw their opportunity and soon the city was thriving with trade up and down the coast to New England and Virginia as well as across the Atlantic.

The Dutch were not alone in exploiting this coast. The Swedish East India Company had founded posts along the Delaware, but in 1655 New Netherland defeated New Sweden and occupied the Swedish stronghold, Fort Christiana (later renamed Wilmington). The British also set their sights on the province, arguing they had a claim from the fifteenth century voyages of John Cabot who explored the region. Furthermore the British and Dutch had become major rivals in trade and had been to war in 1652–4. A plan had been developed for English colonists to attack the New Netherlands, but it was not implemented.

Ten years later King Charles II of England formally annexed New Netherland in response to an alliance of the Dutch and French against England. King Charles granted New Amsterdam and the province to his brother James, who later became King James II, but at that time was Duke of York and Albany. James sent a fleet to attack the colony and on 8 September 1664, Fort Amsterdam surrendered, followed by Fort Orange on 24 September 1664. The settlement of New Amsterdam and the entire colony were renamed New York. Fort Amsterdam was renamed Fort James and Fort Orange became Fort Albany.

The capture of New Netherland led to a second Anglo-Dutch war during 1665–1667, which was partially resolved by the Treaty of Breda in August of 1667 as the Dutch gave up their claim to New Amsterdam in exchange for Surinam (just north of Brazil). After being recaptured by the Dutch once more, and was once again renamed, (this time to New Orange in honour of William of Orange of the Netherlands), the war in Europe went badly for the Dutch. In the Treaty of Westminster in 1674 the province of New Orange was handed back to the British. From that point the British controlled both the city and province of New York. New York City remained the premier British military stronghold in America until the end of the American War of Independence.

OTHER 'YORKS' AROUND THE WORLD

In America there are twenty-seven places called 'York' in twenty-three states across the country. Many of these are tiny places, though a few deserve some attention. The city of York in Pennsylvania was the first capital of the United States, as well as being the birthplace of the Articles of Confederation and the place where the term 'The United States of America' was first spoken. In Nebraska the City of York was founded in 1869 by the South Platte Land company as it lay on the Oregon Trail it was a stopping place for many early pioneers.

Elsewhere in the world the name York is not so common, though there is a small town in Western Australia with the name, which was the first inland European settlement in Western Australia. Although only founded in 1831 it is today classed as a 'Historic Town' and has a claim to be one of the best pre-served historic towns in Australia. On the Australian northern coastline there is a huge tract of land called Cape York which is only accessible during the dry months of April to December

Another Cape York exists in Greenland and it is from there that a massive meteorite has been found which is four and a half billion years old. The huge meteorite is so heavy that for it to be viewed in a New York museum the support structure had to rest on the bedrock. It was removed from Cape York in 1897 by Arctic explorer Robert Peary, but previously the native Inuit people had used the meteorite as a source of iron for knives and other weapons.

In the warmer climates of the West Indies there are three places called York, two in Sierra Leone and two in South Africa, as well as one in Canada and, surprisingly, one in Guatemala.

As well as the single 'York' name, there are many places with York as an element of its name. Two instances of Cape York have also been given, but there are also two instances of York Harbour and York Beach, and one place each called York Factory, York Mills (both in Canada) and York Furnace (in the United States).

As the case of 'New York' shows, there is always the possibility that the place name York was in fact named after the Duke of York rather than the city of York, but the sixteen instances of the place name Yorkshire in the United States is unequivocal in showing the desire of the early settlers to remember their homeland.

APPENDIX THREE

The Heraldry and Civic Regalia of York

The heraldry of York consists of the two classic English symbols, the cross of St George (a red cross on a white background) and five lions. Lions are a feature of the royal coat of arms and three lions were used by Richard I for his coat of arms. It is not possible to accurately date the first use of the York coat of arms, but it probably was devised between 1350–1375, a time when York still held a pre-eminent position because of the Scottish wars.

As well as the coat of arms, the city has a range of historic artefacts, including two swords. The original sword was given to the mayor by Richard II in 1389. It was in use up until 1785 but has since vanished. Today the city uses two other swords. The first is the sword of Sigismund who was the brother-in-law of Richard II. The sword was made for the Emperor Sigismund in 1416 and was originally situated at Windsor Castle, and in 1439 it was given to the city by Henry Hanslap, who was clergyman there. This sword is still carried in state possessions. A second sword was presented to the city by Sir Martin Bowes, Lord Mayor of London, in 1545 to thank the city for sparing St Cuthbert's church in Peaseholme Green from demolition.

Other insignia also have medieval origins and Richard II in 1392 presented the city with a cap and mace, but the cap and mace currently in use date from 1647 and 1915 respectively.

Visitor attractions in York

The Arc   The hand's on archaeology centre where visitors can see and handle archaeological objects and learn how objects were made.

The Castle Museum   The Castle Museum shows the history of everyday life during various historical periods. Kirkgate is the recreated Victorian street within the museum, where visitors can wander in and out of workshops where saddlers, weavers and candle-stick makers worked. The Edwardian period in York is shown in the Half Moon Court. There are also different rooms in the museum showing different periods of time, including domestic interiors from Jacobean, Georgian and Victorian times. The Castle Museum was the prison and prisoner's cells can also be seen. There is a charge for entrance.

City Walls   The city walls are the longest surviving circuit of medieval walls in England being 3.4 kms long. They practically encircle the city centre, although there is a short section where no walls exist because of the presence during medieval times of the King's Fishpool. A walk around the walls lasts a couple of hours. The views from the walls are often stunning, especially on the section behind the Minster between Bootham Bar and Monkgate, and the section between Micklegate and Lendal Bridge. The city walls are free, and are open until dusk every day.

Clifford's Tower   Clifford's Tower is the keep of York Castle and it stands upon the original Norman motte (mound). In 1190 it was the scene of the Jewish Massacre, the most terrible event in the City's history. The present stone keep dates from the thirteenth century after the wooden keep was destroyed by a storm. Clifford's Tower was a Royalist stronghold during the Civil War. The roof was destroyed in 1684 after a fire. There are stunning views of York from on top of the walls. Today Clifford's Tower is operated by English Heritage. There is a charge to get into Clifford's Tower (English Heritage members free).

Ghost Trails   York is reputed to be one of the most haunted cities in Europe. The city's ghostly tales are retold most evenings by a number of ghost walks which are both an enjoyable stroll through the narrow streets and leave the visitor with a sense of unease.

Jorvik Viking Centre   The Jorvik Viking Centre accurately recreates the

203

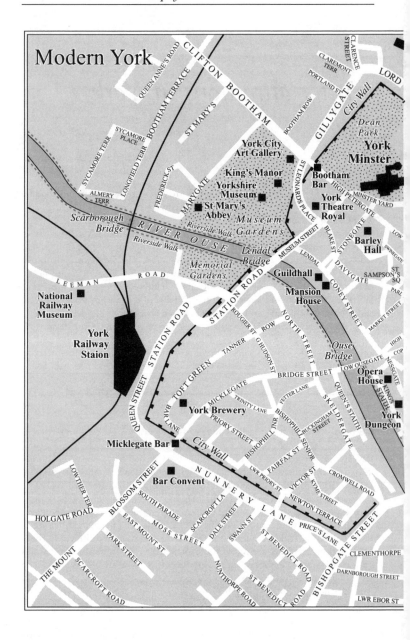

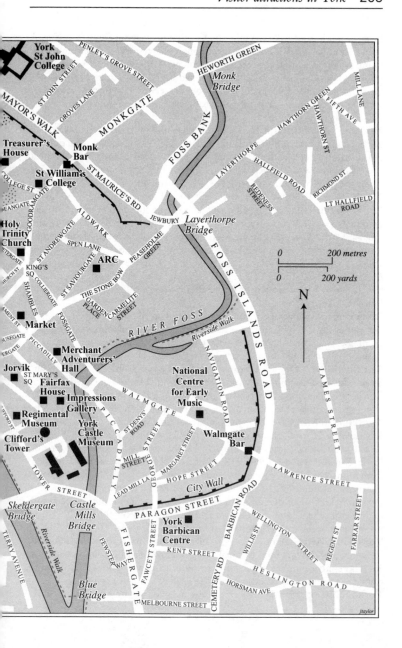

living conditions of Viking York which were uncovered by archaeologists. A visitor 'time capsule' journeys back through the history of York and then journeys round part of the Viking settlement. A bustling street scene, dark, smoky houses and a ship unloading at a wharf have all been recreated – as have the sights, sounds and smells of Jorvik. From the recreated scene the visitor then sees the archaeologists at work and finally many of the ordinary and exotic artefacts uncovered during the excavations.

Merchant Adventurer's Hall   The Merchant Adventurer's Hall is one of the finest guild halls in Europe. Built between 1357–1362 its basic structure has remained unaltered, with a large and impressive upper room, with a hospital and chapel below. There is a collection of portraits and silver, and exhibitions about the Merchant Adventurers. There is a charge for entrance.

The National Railway Museum   The first of the national museums to be located outside London, the National Railway Museum houses the one of the world's largest collections of railway stock and memorabilia, including the original Royal Carriages, Stephenson's Rocket and the Mallard, the fastest steam locomotive in the world. A recent acquisition is the Flying Scotsman which is used for regular steam specials out of York. In the museum the story of the railways is told through a changing programme of exhibitions. There is also the chance to have refreshment in the *Brief Encounter* café on one of the platforms. Entrance is free.

River cruises   There are frequent river cruises up and down the River Ouse during the day. In the warmer summer months there are floodlit cruises in the evenings. The cruises offer an excellent way to see a different view of York. Charges vary depending on the cruise taken.

The Shambles   One of the most photographed and atmospheric streets in York. The street was originally the street of the butchers and is named after the benches (shamels) used to display meat. At one point the upper stories of some buildings are so close together that people on opposite sides can shake hands. The shrine to Margaret Clitheroe is located in the Shambles.

Treasurer's House (National Trust)   The Treasurer's House has a claim to be one of the oddest houses in York. Its last owner, the Victorian industrialist Frank Green, created a house of his dreams, with a medieval hall and then sixteenth to twentieth century decoration in different rooms. It was originally the medieval house of the Treasurer of York Minster, and was built over a Roman road. One of the most famous ghost stories of York's history occurred in the cellar when a group of Roman soldiers walked through the walls. There is a charge for entrance (National Trust members free)

York City Art Gallery   The art gallery houses more than six hundred paintings, and displays both nationally and internationally acclaimed works of art. There are a number of paintings by William Etty – York's most famous painter – and his statue stands outside the Gallery. Entrance is free.

York Dungeon   The Dungeon recreates many of the most bloody and gory

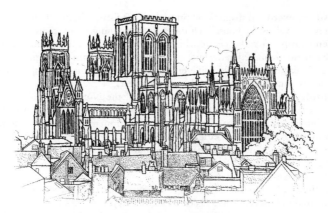

The Minster from the south-east

episodes of York's history, including punishments such as beheading and roasting, and the story of the Gunpowder Plot and the perpetrator's gruesome torture and execution. Not for the faint hearted! There is a charge for entrance.

York Minster The largest Gothic cathedral in England with stunning medieval stained glass. The East Window, showing the creation of the world, is one of the most outstanding examples of the medieval craftsman's art. The exhibition in the crypt tells the story of the Minster. The central tower of the Minster involves a long and tiring climb, but the views across York are spectacular. There is a charge to get into the Minster.

Yorkshire Museum and Museum Gardens The Yorkshire Museum houses the region's finest collections of dinosaurs, as well as Roman, Anglo-Saxon, Viking and medieval treasures. There is also a reconstructed arch from St Mary's Abbey showing the intricate detail of stone carving from the largest Benedictine monastery in the north. The gardens outside the museum contain the remains of St Mary's Abbey. There is a charge for the museum but the Museum Gardens are free.

Places to Visit Outside York

Beningbrough Hall (National Trust) Lying just to the north of York Beningbrough Hall houses part of the National Portrait Gallery's collection of paintings. There are also large grounds and gardens to explore.

Beverley Historic market town with an impressive Minster church, town defences, charming streets and a racecourse.

Castle Howard   A magnificent privately owned stately home of the Howard family. As well as the house itself there are parks and gardens to discover.

Eden Camp   A visitor centre which transports you back to wartime Britain. The museum is housed in the huts of the original Prisoner of War camp built in 1942. Today each hut tells a different story of wartime Britain, complete with the sights, sounds and smells of the wartime years.

Helmsley   Small market town at the foot of the North Yorkshire moors. Helmsley Castle has spectacular earthworks, a twelfth century keep and a range of exhibitions about the social and military issues from medieval times to today.

Fountains Abbey and Studley Royal (National Trust)   A World Heritage Site, the Abbey stands in the majestic grounds of Studley Royal with elegant walks and lakes. At the height of its power the Cistercian Fountains Abbey was one of the wealthiest abbeys in England.

Middleham Castle (English Heritage)   One of Richard III's favourite castles in the midst of the Yorkshire Dales. The Lord Mayor of York visited the castle with presents for Richard III's only son, Edward, Prince of Wales. The castle is now ruinous but gives views over the surrounding countryside.

Murton Museum of Farming   Located just east of York, the farming museum not only contains historic farm equipment, but also reconstructed Iron Age buildings, Roman fort and an entire Viking village. There are also farm animals, an exhibition about bees and working bee hives.

The Yorkshire countryside

Northallerton   County town of North Yorkshire and just to the north of the town is the site of the Battle of the Standard

North York Moors Steam Railway   One of the three longest steam railways in the country with a route of eighteen miles in total through the stunning scenery of the North York Moors

Rievaulx Abbey (English Heritage)   First Cistercian monastic house in Yorkshire. Substantial remains have survived.

Ripon   A charming small cathedral city with large town square and ancient history. The cathedral has an Anglo-Saxon crypt underneath the later, twelfth century, building which stands today.

Royal Armouries Museum, Leeds   The museum houses the national collection of arms and armour, with five themed galleries covering War, Tournament, Self-Defence, Hunting and the arms and armour of the Orient There are spectacular live demonstrations, re-enactments and jousting tournaments – there is even a chance to shoot a crossbow.

Pickering   Small town at the foot of the North York Moors with a large Norman motte and bailey castle. The parish church has excellent medieval murals.

Scarborough   Archetypal Yorkshire coastal resort, with sandy beaches and arcades. Above the town stands Scarborough Castle which dominates the skyline.

Towton   Small village outside York where the Yorkist army, led by Edward IV, gained a decisive victory against the Lancastrian army of Henry VI in 1461.

Yorkshire Air Museum, Elvington   Aviation museum just south-east of York honouring the pilots and station crews who flew from Elvington and further afield

Yorkshire Dales   The Dales are an area of outstanding beauty, with lush green river valleys and upland limestone scenery.

Yorkshire Wolds   Covering most of East Yorkshire the chalk wolds form an undulating and at times spectacular landscape. The Wolds are full of unexpected hidden valleys and almost deserted roads.

Wharram Percy   A fascinating deserted medieval village which contains humps and bumps of medieval dwellings, a large pond and a spectacular ruined church.

Whitby   Site of the original Anglo-Saxon abbey founded by Abbess Hild where the Synod of Whitby was held. It was later refounded after the Norman Conquest by Reinfrid. Today there is an excellent medieval abbey. The town is also a fishing port and has a small beach and some arcades.

Street Names of York

To a tourist it has been rightly said that the street names of York are confusing because the streets are called 'gate' and the gates are called 'Bars'. The street ending 'gate' comes from the Old Norse word for a street 'gata'.

Aldwark   Old English meaning 'old defensive work' and referring to the Roman walls.

Bedern   Old English meaning 'prayer house'.

Bishophill   Either from the Middle English meaning 'Bitch Hill' or 'Bishop's Hill'.

Blake Street   'Blake' comes from the Old Norse meaning 'pale' or 'white'.

Blossom Street   'Blossom' is a corruption of the Old Norse for 'ploughman'.

Bootham   Old Norse meaning 'at the booths'.

Colliergate   Middle English for 'charcoal maker' or 'charcoal dealer'.'

Coney Street   'Coney' is a corruption of the Old Norse for 'kunungr' meaning 'king' and the Anglo-Saxon for street. The name has nothing to do with rabbits.

Coppergate   Old Norse meaning street of the 'turners' or 'joiners', or possibly 'cup' or 'copper'

Davygate   Davy Hall was formerly located in the street. David the Lardiner and his ancestors were clerks of the kitchen for the Forest of Galtres, to the north of York.

Feasegate   Old Norse for the street of the cow-house.

Fetter Lane   Derived from the Middle English for felt maker.

Finkle Street   Still unknown as to what it means though it occurs in many northern towns.

Fishergate   Old Norse meaning street of the 'fisherman'.

Gillygate   Street of the church of St Giles, which was formerly located there.

Goodramgate   Corruption of an Old Norse female name, Guthrun.

Micklegate   Derived from the Old Norse for 'great' or 'large'.

Ogleforth   Probably derived from the Old Norse for 'owl' and the Old English for 'ford'.

Petergate   Named after the St Peter, i.e. the dedication of York Minster.

Shambles   From the Middle English meaning 'flesh benches' and it was the street of the butchers.

Skeldergate   Either the Old Norse for 'shieldmaker', or a 'shelf', as a shelf on the banks of the Ouse.

Spurriergate   Street of the spur makers.

Walmgate   From an Old Norse or Old English female personal name, Walba or Walbi.

Whipmawhopmagate   Possibly associated with whipping, but more likely jokingly to come from 'whitna and whatna' meaning 'what kind of a' street'.

Chronology

BC

55	Romans invade England and leave
54	Second Roman invasion of England

AD

43	Third Roman invasion of England
71	Foundation of York
211	Emperor Septimus Severus died in York
Post 211	Caracalla, Severus's son, made York the provincial capital of *Britannia Inferior* (Lower Britain)
306	Emperor Constantius Chlorus died in York; Constantine proclaimed emperor in York
314	Eborius, bishop of York, summoned to Council of Arles; last reference to York in Roman times
c. 450	Arrival of Angles and Saxons in England
596	Arrival of St Augustine to Canterbury
625	Paulinus arrives at king Edwin of Northumbria's court
627	Date of first mention of York since 314; king Edwin of Northumbria converted to Christianity
633	King Edwin killed in Battle of Hatfield Chase
642	King Oswald killed
664	Synod of Whitby
735	Bede dies; York made into an archbishopric
741	York Minster burned to the ground
782	Alcuin left York for Charlemagne's court
793	Vikings attacked England
866	Vikings captured York
954	Eric Bloodaxe killed
1016	Earl Uhtred of Northumbria killed at Wighill
1066	Battle of Gate Fulford; Battle of Stamford Bridge; Battle of Hastings and Norman Conquest

1068	Normans arrive in York and castle built
1069	Revolt against Normans; Siege raised by William the Conqueror; William the Conqueror held a crown wearing ceremony in York; King Swein of Denmark captured York; William the Conqueror recaptured York; Harrying of the North; Thomas of Bayeux appointed archbishop, starts new Minster
1086	Domesday Book
1138	The Battle of the Standard
1154	Archbishop William FitzHerbert died
1190	Jewish massacre
1212	King John granted a new charter
1217	Hugh Selby became York's first mayor
1227	William Fitzherbert canonised and made a saint
1290	Expulsion of the Jews
1296	Start of the Scottish Wars
1298	Edward I moved the Exchequer and Chancery to York for the first time
1312	Abolition of the Knights Templar
1319	Scottish raid kills the mayor of York
1328	King Edward III and Philippa of Hainault married in York Minster
1338	Government departments left York for the last time
1349–50	The Black Death
1381	The Peasant's Revolt
1405	Archbishop Scrope 'martyred'
1461	Battle of Towton
1465	Archbishop Neville's feast
1485	Battle of Bosworth
1530	Cardinal Wolsey, archbishop of York, dies
1536	Dissolution of the smaller monasteries; Pilgrimage of Grace
1539	Dissolution of the larger monasteries
1546–7	Closure of chantries and religious guilds
1586	Martyrdom of Margaret Clitheroe
1605	The Gunpowder Plot
1642–46	English Civil War
1644	Siege of York; Battle of Marston Moor
1651	George Fox thrown down the steps of the Minster
1688	The Glorious Revolution
1715	Jacobite Rebellion
1739	Dick Turpin hanged in York
1745	Second Jacobite Rebellion
1796	Foundation of the Retreat

1829	Jonathan Martin burned the Minster
1832	Cholera epidemic
1836	Police force in York created
1847	Fall from grace of George Hudson, the Railway King
1849	Queen Victoria's only official visit to York
1899–1902	Boer War
1901	Death of Queen Victoria
1914–18	First World War
1916	Three Zeppelin raids on York
1926	The General Strike
1939–45	The Second World War
1942	Most serious German air-raid on York
1951	Festival of the Arts
1963	Foundation of the University of York
1969	Lord Esher's report
1974	Local government reorganisation
1975	National Railway Museum opened
1984	York Minster fire
1985	Jorvik Viking Centre opened
2000	Severe flooding

Further Reading

Attreed, L.C., *The York House Books* (York, 1991)

Aylmer, G.E. and Cant, R *A History of York Minster* (Oxford 1979)

Barnwell, P.S., Cross C., and Rycraft, A. *Mass and Parish in late Medieval England: The Use of York (Reading 2005)*

Brown, S., York Minster: An Architectural History, *c.*1220–1500, (London, 1993)

Drake, Francis *Eboracum* (York, 1736)

Hall, R., *The English Heritage Book of York* (London, 1998)

Hall, R., *The English Heritage Book of Viking Age York* (London, 1994)

Hallett, M., and Rendall, J., (eds) *Eighteenth-Century York: Culture, Space and Society* (York, 2003)

Johnson, A.F., and Rogerson, M., (eds) York (Records of Early English Drama Series) (Toronto, 1979)

Lilley, J.M., et al 'The Jewish Burial Ground at Jewbury', *The Medieval Cemeteries, The Archaeology of York* 12/3 (York, 1994)

Kightly, C., and Semlyen, R., *Lords of the City* (York 1980)

Murray, Hugh et al *York Through the Eyes of the Artist* (York, 1990)

Murray, H., Photographs and Photographers of York: The Early Years, 1844–79 (York, 1986)

Norton, C., St William of York, (York, 2006)

Nuttgens, P., (ed) *History of the City of York* (Pickering, 2001)

Ottaway, P., *The English Heritage Book of Roman York* (London, 1993)

Palliser, D., *Tudor York* (Oxford 1979)

Peacock, A.J., *York in the Great War 1914–1918* (York 1993)

Pevsner, N., *Yorkshire: York and the East Riding* (London 1995)

Rees Jones, Sarah (ed) *The Government of Medieval York* (York, 1995)

Rowntree, B.S., *Poverty, a Study in Town Life* (London 1901)

Royal Commission on Historic Monuments, An Inventory of Historic Monuments in the City of York, Vols I, II, III, IV, V (London, 1972–1981)

Stacpoole, A., (ed) *The Noble City of York* (York 1972)

Tillot, P. M., (ed) (1961) *The Victoria History of the Counties of England. A History of Yorkshire: The City of York* (Oxford, 1961)
White, E., (ed) *Feeding the City: York* (Totness, 2000)

Journals and other publications

Borthwick papers (York, two a year)
Fasicules of York Archaeological Trust (York, internittent)
York Civic Trust (York, annual reports)
York Historian (York, annual journal)
Yorkshire Archaeological Society Record Series
Yorkshire Archaeological Journal

Index

A TRAVELLER'S HISTORY OF CYPRUS

Tim Boatswain

Comment on *A Traveller's History of Greece* co-authored by Tim Boatswain
'*Clearly written, well-structured, and fixing on illuminating and arresting details about events, places, and participants, the book packs a lot into a compact format . . . [An] excellent, needed, and rewarding publication.*'
SMALL PRESS

Over two million visitors a year visit Cyprus and this new Traveller's History retells the complete story of the island's past and also touches on the sensitive present-day issues for both sides of the island. As always the retelling of the island's story will help visitors understand its present situation and guide them to the heritage sites.

Although Cyprus is a relatively small island, its position in the East Mediterranean has always given it a strategic importance beyond its size. Well placed for travel from all over the globe with plenty of sunshine throughout the year – Cyprus has become a favoured tourist destination. All visitors, whether to the Greek or Turkish side of the island discover that Cyprus has an immensely rich history as a result of so many different civilisations making their mark upon its people. The book includes historical maps, a Gazetteer and a Chronology.

Tim Boatswain is Pro Vice-Chancellor at the University of Huddersfield and has degrees in archaeology and anthropology. He is a regular visitor to the island and publishes and lectures on the history of Cyprus.

A TRAVELLER'S HISTORY OF GREECE

Timothy Boatswain and Colin Nicolson

The many facets of Greece are presented in this unique book.

In *A Traveller's History of Greece*, the reader is provided with an authoritative general history of Greece from its earlier beginnings down to the present day. It covers in a clear and comprehensive manner the classical past, the conflict with Persia, the conquest by the Romans, the Byzantine era and the occupation by the Turks; the struggle for Independence and the turbulence of recent years, right up to current events.

This history will help the visitor make sense of modern Greece against the background of its diverse heritage. A Gazetteer, cross-referenced with the main text highlights the importance of sites, towns and ancient battlefields. A Chronology details the significant dates and a brief survey of the artistic styles of each period is given. Illustrated with maps and line drawings *A Traveller's History of Greece* is an invaluable companion for your holiday.

A TRAVELLER'S HISTORY OF ITALY

Valerio Lintner

In *A Traveller's History of Italy* the author analyses the development of the Italian people from pre-historic times right through to the imaginative, resourceful and fiercely independent Italians we know today.

All of the major periods of Italian history are dealt with, including the Etruscans, the Romans, the communes and the city states which spawned the glories of the Renaissance. In more modern times, Unification and the development and regeneration of the Liberal state into Fascism are covered, as well as the rise of Italy to the position it currently enjoys as a leading member of the European Community.

The Gazetteer, which is cross-referenced to the main text, highlights sites, towns, churches and cathedrals of historical importance for the visitor.

A TRAVELLER'S HISTORY OF INDIA

SinhaRajah Tammita-Delgoda

'For anyone ... planning a trip to India, the latest in the excellent Traveller's History series ... provides a useful grounding for those whose curiosity exceeds the time available for research.' **The London Evening Standard**

India is heir to one of the world's oldest and richest civilizations and the origin of many of the ideas, philosophies and movements which have shaped the destiny of humankind.

For the traveller, India is both an inspiration and a challenge. The sheer wealth of Indian culture has fascinated generations of visitors. We see the sweeping panorama of Indian history, from the ancient origins of Hinduism, Jainism, Buddhism, and the other great religions, through the tumultuous political history of India's epic struggle against colonialism, to the ravages of Partition, Non-Alignment, and finally the emergence of India as a powerful modern state still grounded in the literature and culture of an ancient land. *A Traveller's History of India* covers the whole scope of India's past and present history and allows the reader to make sense of what they see in a way that no other guide book can.

A TRAVELLER'S HISTORY OF ENGLAND

Christopher Daniell

A Traveller's History of England gives a comprehensive and enjoyable survey of England's past from prehistoric times right through to the 1990s.

All the major periods of English history are dealt with, including the Roman occupation, and the invasions of the Anglo-Saxons, Vikings and Normans, and the power struggles of the medieval kings. The Reformation, the Renaissance and the Civil War are discussed, as well as the consequences of the Industrial Revolution and urbanism, and the establishment of an Empire which encompassed a quarter of the human race. In this century the Empire has been transformed into the Commonwealth, two victorious, but costly, World Wars have been fought, the Welfare State was established, and membership of the European Union was finally achieved.

Illustrated throughout with maps and line drawings, *A Traveller's History of England* offers an insight into the country's past and present and is an invaluable companion for all those who want to know more about a nation whose impact upon the rest of the world has been profound.

A TRAVELLER'S HISTORY OF SCOTLAND

Andrew Fisher

'. . . the book is an extremely enjoyable journey through our nation's past.'

A Traveller's History of Scotland begins with Scotland's first people and their culture. Before the Vikings in 900 it was a land of romantic kingdoms and saints, gradually overtaken by more pragmatic struggles for power. Centuries of strife lead up to the turbulent years of Mary Queen of Scots, the Calvinistic legacy of Knox, and the bitterness of final defeat.

The dreams of the Jacobites are contrasted with the cruel reality of the end of the Stuarts and the Act of Union with England. Scotland now saw an age of industry and despoliation. The result was much emigration and an obsession with the nation's past which glorified the legends of the Highlander and the Clans. In this century, the loss of identity and drift to the south have been followed by a new surge of national pride with higher aspirations for the future. In the millenium the effects of devolution and a separate Scottish parliament are eagerly awaited.

A Traveller's History of Scotland explains the roots of Scottish history and is an invaluable companion for visitors.

A TRAVELLER'S HISTORY OF IRELAND

Peter Neville

A Traveller's History of Ireland gives a full and accurate portrait of Ireland from Prehistory right up to the 1990s.

Hundreds of thousands of tourists visit Ireland every year drawn by the landscape, the people and the underlying atmosphere created by its rich heritage.

The story opens with mysterious early Celtic Ireland where no Roman stood, through Saint Patrick's mission to Ireland which began the process of making it 'an island of saints', to the struggle with Viking and Irish enemies alike.

It moves through the arrival of the Norman 'Strongbow' in the twelfth century, and the beginnings of the difficult and tragic Anglo-Irish relationship. Great historical figures like Hugh O'Neill, Cromwell, and Jonathan Swift figure as well as ordinary people like the Londonderry 'apprentice boys; who helped change the course of Irish history. Then into modern times with the great revolts of 1798, the horrors of the Potato Famine and the careers of the leading constitutional nationalists, O'Connell and Parnell. The book ends with a description of modern Ireland, and of its two separate Catholic Nationalist and Protestant Unionist traditions.

A TRAVELLER'S HISTORY OF VENICE

Peter Mentzel

The glorious city of Venice is now seen as a prime tourist destination, but behind its lovely facade lies a fascinating historical story. *A Traveller's History of Venice* presents a concise and entertaining overview from the fifth century to the perils of flood and tourism that face Venice today.

The main theme is the unique place that Venice has occupied in the history of Europe in general and Italy in particular. While Venice has been politically part of a united Italy since 1866, its development tied it as much to the Eastern Mediterranean and the Levant as to the Italian peninsula. It is this diverse cultural mix which has made Venice such a fascinating, even magical place.

There are special reference features on the islands in the lagoon, the history of the gondola, Venice's main churches, galleries and museums. Through anecdote and information *A Traveller's History of Venice* allows every reader to enjoy the riches and quirks of this unique city.

A TRAVELLER'S HISTORY OF MEXICO

Kenneth Pearce

Mexico has a long and colourful history with a many-layered cultural heritage. In this definitive book the author offers an expert account of the country from its earliest civilisations right up to the present day.

A Traveller's History of Mexico begins with life before the first elite groups of the Olmecs and Mayans emerged. Their culture was finally subsumed into the mighty Aztec Empire. There is a full and vivid account of life under the Aztecs – a civilisation that in its turn was tragically ended by the arrival of the Spanish conquistador Hernan Cortes. The crushing burden of colonial rule driven by the forces of greed and oppression led to centuries of unrest.

In the nineteenth century, the War of Independence led to the founding of the Mexican Republic.The next two hundred years of Mexico's story are peopled with larger than life characters such as the Emperor Maximilian and his tragic wife, Carlota,General Anna, Emiliano Zapata and Pancho Villa. The author ends his survey with a portrait of a country under a new president facing the problems of a rising population, drugs, corruption and the disenchanted Indian population.

A TRAVELLER'S HISTORY OF SOUTH-EAST ASIA

J.M Barwise & N.J.White

A mass tourist industry arose in South East Asia from the 1960s. Yet, travellers from the rest of Asia and Europe have been visiting the region for centuries, attracted by its rich diversity of cultures, peoples and scenery. From the early Christian era in Europe, South East Asia was known as the 'Land of Gold'. *A Traveller's History of South East Asia* is a lucid and concise introduction to the histories of the modern states of Malaysia, Indonesia, Vietnam, Cambodia, Laos, Thailand, Singapore, Brunei and East Timor, providing an essential guide for both tourists and the general reader. It spans the history of the region from 'Java Man' some one million years ago to the development of the high-tech, sky-scraper cities of the new millennium.

Following chapters on the physical environment and the earliest human history of South East Asia, the authors carry the reader through the classical kingdoms that produced such architectural marvels as Borobudur in Java and Angkor Wat in Cambodia. The book further explores South East Asia's growing trade with the outside world from 1500 culminating in colonisation by the European imperial powers in the nineteenth and twentieth centuries.

A TRAVELLER'S HISTORY OF PORTUGAL

Ian Robertson

A definitive concise history of Portugal by an author once described as 'the Elizabeth David of travel writers'. It was not until the twelfth century that Portugal became a country in its own right, having been a Roman colony and then having suffered both Barbarian and Islamic invasions.

Long referred to as being 'Britain's oldest ally', but often placed in the shade of Spain, Portugal deserves equal attention.

The golden age of discoveries, the reign and foresight of Henry the Navigator and great seamen such as Vasco da Gama led to the founding of Portugal's empire and wealth. Troubled times followed: in 1755 Lisbon was virtually levelled by the 'Great Earthquake', and the country had hardly recovered its former prosperity when it was overrun by Napoleon's troops at the start of the Peninsular War, to be followed not long after by the Miguelite civil war. The middle decades of the nineteenth century saw the Port Wine trade flourishing, and further expansion into Africa.

During the last quarter of the twentieth century, ever since the bloodless revolution of 1974 overthrew the right-wing dictatorship of Salazar, the country has regained its stability, and now takes its rightful place in the European Community.

CHASTLETON TRAVEL an imprint of Arris Publishing Ltd
12 Main Street, Adlestrop
Moreton-in-Marsh
Gloucestershire GL56 0YN

Tel: 01608 658758
Fax: 01608 659345

To order any title price £9.99 plus £1.00 postage within UK
Please phone or email info@arrisbooks.com